THE CENTRAL SCHOOL OF SPEECH AND DRAMA

UNIVERSITY OF LONDON

Please return or renew this item by the last date shown.

GILDED BUTTERFLIES

GILDED BUTTERFLIES

THE RISE AND FALL
OF THE LONDON SEASON

Philippa Pullar

HAMISH HAMILTON
LONDON

First published in Great Britain 1978
by Hamish Hamilton Ltd
90 Great Russell Street, London WC1B 3PT

Copyright © 1978 by Philippa Pullar

Design by Patrick Leeson

British Library Cataloguing in Publication Data

Pullar, Philippa
    Gilded butterflies.
    1. Upper classes—England—London—History
    2. London—Social life and customs
    I. Title
    942.1   DA688

    ISBN 0-241-89965-6

Filmset and printed in Great Britain by
BAS Printers Limited, Over Wallop, Hampshire

For Guy

Acknowledgments

I would like to acknowledge the help of my
editors Christopher Sinclair-Stevenson and Anne
Gray (who found all the illustrations); also the
help of Mr Peter Townend, Mr Douglas
Matthews and the staff of the London Library,
the library staff of the British Museum, Mr
Michael Holroyd and Mr Simon Seligman for
their suggestions, and Miss Virginia Bell who did
a great deal of research for this book and who
also wrote some of it.

The Publishers wish to thank the Mansell
Collection for permission to reproduce the
illustrations on pages 14, 17, 21, 22, 24, 26, 28,
30, 33, 39, 43, 44, 46, 49, 50, 52, 54, 57, 58, 61,
63, 64, 69, 71(*l*), 73, 80, 86, 88, 101, 103, 109,
116, 118; the Radio Times Hulton Picture Library
for pages 19, 41, 45, 71(*r*), 79, 83, 97, 104, 105,
120, 122, 125, 127, 131, 132, 140, 144, 151, 154,
158, 159, 173, 175; the Mary Evans Picture
Library for pages 2, 75, 77, 84, 92, 94, 102, 106,
108, 115, 152, 156; Keystone Press for pages 181,
183, 184, 185; Sotheby's Belgravia (photographs
by Cecil Beaton) for pages 165, 167, 168, 169; the
Bettman Archive for pages 135, 138, 143; the
British Museum for pages 10, 100, 111;
Popperfoto for pages 90, 187; the National
Portrait Gallery for pages 35, 37; Mrs Barbara
Cartland for pages 162, 171; Fox Photos for page
166; Barry Swaebe for page 189; Associated Press
for page 147; Lady de Lisle for page 20; Service
de Documentation Photographique for page 67;
Photographie Bulloz for page 113.

So we'll live,
And pray, and sing, and tell old tales, and laugh
At gilded butterflies, and hear poor rogues
Talk of court news; and we'll talk with them too,
Who loses and who wins; who's in, who's out;

King Lear (V.iii.8)

Introduction

WHEN I came out in 1953 the London season had already deteriorated into being a cynical marriage market. My mother remembers looking over the banisters in Grosvenor House at us all practising our curtsey to that ridiculous cake. 'Isn't it sad,' one of the other mothers said, 'there they are *en route* to the kitchen sink.' It was assumed that one's mission was to get married. Education was not important for a girl, or so my mother believed (which was just as well since I was always being expelled from my schools, together with my pony which chased the riding mistress up a tree). So apart from Madame Vacani's curtsey lessons—ready for the great day of presentation—I learnt remarkably little. One establishment I never attended was the Cygnets which gave lessons in opening bazaars, running social functions and looking elegant—all believed to be essential to a young lady's education.

Though unschooled in public speaking I still managed, as a result of the Season, to get engaged, to a lovely man with a lovely house. He died. About five years later I married, having met my husband with friends I had made through the Season. The marriage—like many of my friends' and contemporaries'—ended in divorce. Nevertheless in those days the Season did have a function. After our segregated school days it provided a means—albeit an expensive one—of meeting people. Now of course there is very little point. Many schools are co-ed; people start smoking, drinking and going to parties and dances when they are thirteen; and with the pill plenty of girls are sleeping with boys by the time they are sixteen.

We certainly behaved ourselves badly, although not in bed—it was sillier than that. Newspapers loved reporting incidents of police arriving at parties where we unchaperoned debs and our 'delights' were hurling champagne and eggs and bacon into the gutters below. 'Disgraceful,' the older generation would mutter. 'It could never have happened in the old days.' How wrong they were! London has always had a disastrous effect on people. For hundreds of years the upper classes have been flinging drink about—and doing much worse besides. The idea of a straight-laced Season belonging to the nineteenth century is also a mistaken one It had begun by the turn of the seventeenth and the marriage market was only part of—just as the London Season was only part of—a whole system rooted in the country. The nobility would arrive in London to go to court and, released from their country responsibilities, many would behave in the wildest ways. The saying 'drunk as a lord' is no fiction. Over and again it would be reiterated: the nobleman's place and duty lay in the country. Nevertheless the aristocracy have swarmed to London and dissipated their health and their fortunes from one Elizabethan era to another.

Professor Hexter has suggested that a way to review English history would be by examining the changing role of the aristocracy from century to century. This book is not designed to be a history: yet it is impossible to write about the rise and fall of the Season without considering the ways in which the aristocracy has adjusted itself and its relation to the Court and Crown. Its values, its manners and its morals have been influenced by social upheaval and especially by other countries, notably France and America.

Queen Elizabeth I embodied unity, security, continuity and glory.

Chapter 1

FIRST it is important to understand the function of the Crown, the Court and the Aristocracy. These days the hierarchical system is looked on as some curious relic to be filed under such labels as 'stratification'. Academics, especially American ones, treat it as a subject for theses (and even debutantes come under sociological scrutiny). In fact the aristocratic system operated simply. The feudal Lord of the Manor was also Lord of the Soil. His wealth came basically from his land which he held from the monarch and in return he sat in Parliament whenever summoned and took his retainers to fight when called. He also carried the special responsibility of having the land worked, governing his neighbourhood in the monarch's name, managing and cherishing his family, maintaining a household of servants and keeping table for labourers and guests—which could mean that he supported hundreds of relations, retainers and servants.

Sir William Holles, for example, kept open house in the sixteenth century from All Hallows to Candlemas during which time any gentleman could stay for three days without being asked to explain himself; and the Earl of Shrewsbury's household consumed in one September week 23 sheep and lambs, 2 bullocks, 1 veal, 59 chickens, capon and pullets, 5 pigs, 24 pigeons and 54 rabbits, and drank 750–1,250 gallons of wine—the beer consumption being 5–8 pints per person per day.

The prevailing temper of the sixteenth century is an antithesis to our puritanical twentieth-century ethic. Until the second half of the nineteenth century England ran on a patriarchal aristocratic principle, maintaining as essential values generous hospitality, class distinction and patronage, while being indifferent to the sins of the flesh—provided certain conditions were adhered to. People did not earn wealth so much as win it. If one attracted the

Queen's eye and gained her favour one might be rewarded by being sent off on commissions. The only way to promotion lay at court, which was the centre of everything: government, power, pleasure, intrigue and scandal. Ambitious men congregated there to make marriages, seek office and enjoy themselves in a whirl of balls and tournaments, pageants and banquets, so that by 1560 half the peerage had London houses. Some lived splendidly along the banks of the Thames in palaces appropriated from various bishops; others had settled in priories and friaries, haunted sometimes by their former inhabitants. Legend has it that the Duke and Duchess of Suffolk were pacing the Gothic gallery of what had been a Carthusian monastery in Sheen when a skeleton's arm suddenly shot out of the wall barring their way with an axe dripping with blood.

For health reasons the court moved along the banks of the Thames from one palace to another—Richmond, Windsor, Greenwich, Eltham and Westminster. Here the palace of Whitehall lay for nearly half a mile beside the river, a warren of galleries, apartments, gardens, tennis courts, tilt yard and bowling green. In winter the chambers were redolent with musk and fragrant waters. In summer they were strewn with birch branches, roses, marigolds, lavender and sweet herbs. It was a world of shining fabrics, glittering jewels and music. Trumpeters and kettledrummers wore bright cloaks with brilliant facings; gay ribbons and gold banners streamed from their instruments. The Yeomen of the Guard were clothed in scarlet, golden roses embroidered on their backs. Wax lights flickered on Persian and Indian carpets, tapestries, silver bed-covers lined with ermine, ash- and straw-coloured satins, silks studded with coral, pearl and black onyx, ropes of milky pearls and necklaces of gold scallop shells encrusted with diamonds— the more things cost the more they were esteemed.

At the centre and most magnificent of all was the Queen. Her function was both practical and metaphysical. Her body was precious, bestowed with the power of healing. Her incandescent skin encapsulated those symbols of mystical significance, magic, fertility, god and warrior. She embodied unity, security, continuity and glory. Her power was absolute. Nothing could be had without her approbation—and even with it things were far from certain, for Elizabeth was notoriously stingy with her handouts. One could emerge wonderfully rewarded as a Master of the Horse, a Leicester, or one might find oneself slinking back to the country ruined. Many an ageing courtier was to be seen lurking in the draughty passages, fawning and flattering, doffing the faded plumes of his cap.

Nowadays the Elizabethan courtier is held up as an ideal of chivalry. His role was to spend lavishly and dress brilliantly—extravagance was not a vice but a virtue and his success was judged by the richness of his clothes, jewels and attendants. He must also have a reasonable knowledge of public affairs and be able to perform gracefully on horse, the tennis court, the fencing piste and the dance floor—especially the dance floor. The Queen's attention was drawn to most of her favourites while they were dancing. Leicester had beautiful legs and he executed his steps so marvellously that one dance was called after him; the Earl of Oxford, who was so good-looking that all the Maids of Honour fell in love with him, won Elizabeth's favour with his fine leaps, and so did Sir Christopher Hatton.

Court masques were an essential part of life. The Renaissance believed in the power of idealism and art. Imagination was seen as a power to control and order the world, change and subdue men. Thus the masque was a celebration and an allegory expressing the obligations of royalty and creating heroic roles for the leaders of society, the monarch at the centre depicted as some exemplary figure, Solomon (Wisdom), Neptune (tamer of the elements), Pan (God of nature) and so on. The image of the monarch was essential. He was hero of court and culture, god of peace and wisdom, transforming Winter to Spring, making the earth fruitful and taming the universe. The theory was: what the audience watched they would ultimately become. In any case with their wonderful clothes and jewels the audience were all part of the show, living emblems of the aristocratic hierarchy. The royal seat was often set directly on the stage—for not only must the monarch see the play but he must be seen beholding it. Then the closer one sat to the monarch the better it was, an index to one's status or the degree of favour one enjoyed. The climactic moment of most masques was nearly always the same, the fiction would open outwards to include the whole court, the masquers would descend from the stage and take partners from the audience for the court ball.

'We princes I tell you are set on stages in the sight and view of all the world duly observed,' the Queen said, and Elizabethan court life was itself a masquerade. The simplest matters were surrounded by ritual and symbols. Hentzner describes laying the dinner table. First a gentleman entered bearing a rod, then another with a tablecloth, both kneeled three times in veneration, spread the table and, kneeling again, retired. Two others, one with the rod again, the other with a salt cellar, a plate and bread, kneeled as before, then placed them on the table; then entered one unmarried lady and one married, bearing a tasting knife. The former dressed in white prostrated herself three times, approached the table and rubbed the plates with bread and salt. Then the Yeomen of the Guard entered bareheaded bringing in at each turn a

OVERLEAF: Plan of Whitehall Palace.

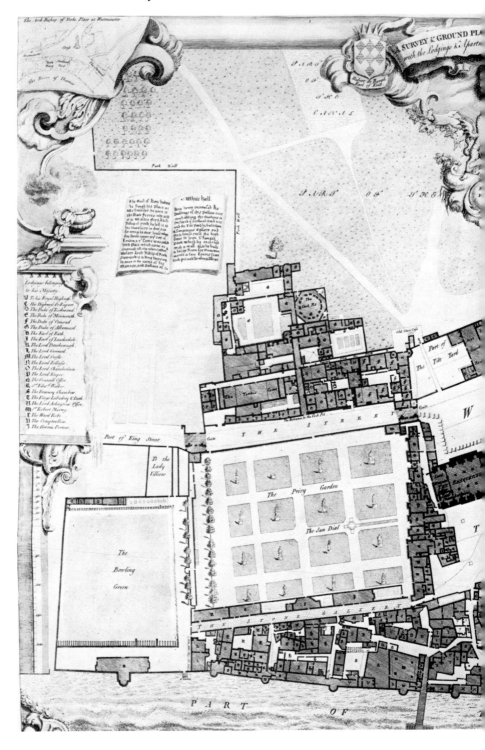

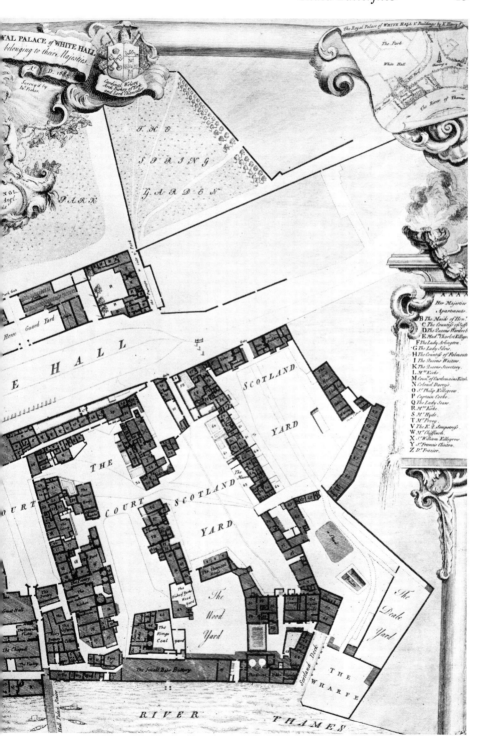

course of twenty-four dishes served on plate, most of it gilt. The dishes were received by a gentleman in the same order as they were brought and placed upon the table, the lady taster giving to each of the guard a mouthful in case of poison. During all this time twelve trumpets and two kettledrums made the hall ring for half an hour together. At the end of the ceremony a number of unmarried ladies appeared, lifted the meat off the table and conveyed it to the Queen's inner chamber.

When the Queen's court went abroad it was in strict procession. The Lord Chamberlain would go first, followed by all the nobility who were at court and the Knights of the Order who were present walked near the Queen before whom six heralds bore maces. After her marched the Gentlemen of the Guard, each carrying a halberd and after them the Maids of Honour all sumptuously attired. The fronts of the houses by which the procession passed would be covered with tapestry, arras and cloth of gold and there would be the ringing of bells and music. At various stages buildings were erected representing castles, palaces, rocks and forests, and nymphs, fauns, satyrs, gods, goddesses, angels and devils would appear with giants, savages, dragons, saints, knights, buffoons and dwarfs, reciting, most of them, odes in praise of the Queen.

This glittering court had a purpose—it attracted foreign visitors and young talent and drew the more unruly nobles into an arena where they could be distracted from such expensive diversions as riot and rebellion. The court sparkled especially during the numerous negotiations for the Queen's hand in marriage. This was a subject that exercised her ministers during the whole of her child-bearing life. A child from the Queen's body was required to ensure succession. Her body, her health and the prospects of her fertility were discussed far and wide. But the Queen was sexually complicated. The paraphernalia of diplomatic courtings was delicious to her, amorous skirmishing one of her favourite delights. But she would not, could not be married, not to Essex, not even to Leicester. As she grew older, younger suitors stepped forward. At the age of thirty-seven there was Anjou, aged twenty-one; at forty, the youngest son of Catharine of Medici, also aged twenty-one, whom she nicknamed The Frog. At his visit a banqueting pavilion was constructed of canvas, elaborately painted to resemble stone; 292 glass windows were let into the walls, the roof was painted with clouds, stars, suns and sunrays; wreaths of holly, ivy and rue were hung everywhere and baskets of pomegranates, oranges, cucumbers and grapes were sprayed with gold. Yet again it all came to nothing.

Elizabeth I reflected the magnificence of her court.

All through her reign rumours flew about and people were arrested for saying that she slept with Leicester, with Sir Christopher Hatton, with others besides. Certainly both Hatton and Leicester longed to marry her. A terrible scandal blew up when Leicester's wife, Amy Robsart, was discovered at the bottom of the stairs with her neck broken. The Queen, it was said, was going to marry her horsekeeper, who had killed his wife. But she was virginity personified and she made a performance of it. Once when she entertained some French nobles who had escorted Mary, Queen of Scots, she devised a ballet to be danced on the Eve of the Nativity of the Virgin in a certain chamber at Greenwich, hung with a set of tapestries depicting the wise and foolish virgins. She (who was born under the sign of Virgo) danced with her Maids of Honour (who anyway were supposed to be virgins) in the Chamber of the Virgin.

Marriage was the spring of the system. One prayed that God would provide an heir to inherit the title and the land. Much energy went into catching heiresses and making matches, which were generally concocted when the children were a few years old, and contracted when the girl reached twelve or thirteen. The bride and bridegroom would be seen into bed together and sewn into their sheets by the wedding party. There was no honeymoon. The wife was usually sent home and the husband would resume his education. Court was the only place where girls could escape parental vigilance. But it was not easy with the Queen being so sexually inhibited. If they asked permission to marry they were beaten and rebuffed; if they married secretly and were found out the husband was imprisoned and if they waited until the girl was pregnant they were *both* liable to be imprisoned. Poor Mary Shelton who married Mr Scudamore was dealt so liberally with blows by Her Majesty that her finger was broken—which was officially caused by a falling candlestick.

'Marry thy daughters in time lest they marry themselves,' Lord Burghley once advised. In the case of his favourite daughter, Ann Cecil, he married her to the handsome Earl of Oxford, laying on lavish celebrations and a marriage feast that lasted three days. But Oxford was an awful husband. He tormented his bride, left her lonely in the country while he frolicked at court and finally had four children by her, all of which Lord Burghley had to bring up. Girls did sometimes rebel. Lady Cave of Stanford arranged for her daughter, Nell, to marry Sir William Cavendish and was so furious when the girl confessed the evening before that she was secretly engaged to Sir George Beeston that she 'drew her by the hair out of the house'. Many men found themselves obliged to run into debt the moment they came into their inheritance in order to furnish their houses. Furniture, beds, hangings, plate, coaches and other

Robert Dudley, Earl of Leicester, the Queen's Master of the Horse.

The Queen and Leicester executing fine leaps.

household goods were part of a man's personal estate. In 1585 the Earl of Northumberland found himself 'soe well left for moveables as was not worthe a fyer shovell or a paire of tongs what was left me was wainscotts or things rivetted with nales, for wyfes commonly are great scratchers after there husband's death if things be loose'.

Every summer the court left London and wandered off into the country on progress. These manoeuvres, which were like the movement of small armies, had two purposes, namely to show the Queen off to her subjects and for her to sample their hospitality. It was to accommodate these hordes, which consisted of servants, government departments, foreign embassies, peers and peeresses and various hangers-on, that courtiers vied with each other to build such houses as Theobalds, Hatfield and Audley End.

The royal visit was an expensive honour (the Queen visited Hatfield three times, each stay costing between two and three thousand pounds) and one that some preferred not to receive. Because of Elizabeth's notorious inability to make up her mind each summer everyone's nerves were on edge as

Reputedly Elizabeth I in fancy dress.

Edward Vere, Earl of Oxford, so good-looking that all
the Maids of Honour fell in love with him.

rumours spread through the country regarding the approach of Her Majesty. Letters would be dispatched to friends advising their immediate departure to London, but flight was not always effective. In 1601 the Queen decided to drop in on the Earl of Lincoln in Chelsea. He was not at home and his servants, presumably under instruction, refused to let her in. She was furious. She *would* dine there. The Earl of Northumberland and Sir Robert Cecil thought it prudent to arrange a succulent feast, leaving the absent host to foot the bill. Lincoln was no advertisement for chivalry. There is a story of his quarrelling with a neighbour in Chelsea and in revenge stacking a load of nightsoil on a wharf just where the fumes would cause maximum nuisance. Others could also behave childishly and forget themselves. Henry Howard, 2nd Viscount Bindon, on meeting the Sheriff of Dorset, repeatedly galloped past him splashing him with mud and then knocked his hat into a puddle. Lord Bergavenny struck the Earl of Oxford and drew blood in the Presence Chamber and the Earl of Oxford, as he was bowing to the Queen, farted.

Most courtiers had finer control, and unlike churlish Lincoln looked on Her Majesty's visit as an investment for the future, which might pay dividends. On the other hand it might not. As the Queen grew older she became more avaricious and needed the reassurance of more expensive presents and more extravagant allegorical performances. Armies of nymphs, fauns and satyrs singing sweet songs would emerge from 'delicate bowres' all over England. The golden eyes would gaze out on dancing, banquets, hunting and bull-baiting, and then her loyal subjects would advance offering nosegays of diamonds and pearls, embroidered dresses and cloaks, presented with the assistance of Sylvanus, Mars, Bacchus, Ceres, Neptune, etc.

With such extravagance many of the aristocracy's incomes and land holdings deteriorated and as a result so did respect for their titles. When Leicester died in 1588 he owed several thousand pounds to over fifty tradesmen for plate, lace, embroidery, jewels, fur, cloth, trumpets, beer pots, groceries, mending of musical instruments and repair of tents. When Lord Willoughby d'Eresby was promoted to Lieutenant-General of the English forces in 1589 his secretary reckoned that he had spent £7,689 before and during the siege of Bergen. His woods were cut down, his stock sold off, his land mortgaged, his plate and his wife's jewels pawned. Even so his debts were at least £4,000. All this despite the capture and ransoming of two rich prisoners and despite his official pay and perquisites.

As for the Earl of Essex it has been suggested that it was his debts and the nagging of his creditors which drove him to the act of folly which was to cost him his life. Despite royal grants of land, cash and monopolies, his outgoings

The Queen and her court on a Progress.

Robert Devereux, Earl of Essex.

exceeded his income. His style of living, his assiduous cultivation of a huge clientele to support his political position, his heavy personal expenditure on military expeditions all contrived to run him into debt. The New Year was a special present-giving time. According to de Maisse, the French Ambassador, all the peers and peeresses of the realm, the bishops, the chief officers of state, the Queen's household servants including the apothecary and the pastry cook, all had to present her with tokens of their loyalty. The ambassador lists an inventory of goods which included jewels, money, petticoats, silk stockings, scented gloves, looking glasses, fans, bracelets, caskets studded with precious stones, books, bibles, jars of green ginger and lemon rinds, meat knives, lozenges and pies made of peaches and quinces.

Poor Philip Sidney, who is often held up as the perfect example of an Elizabethan gentleman, was always short of money, his finances being strained by his court wardrobe and the entertainments he gave to honour the Queen. For the two-day pageant which he shared with the Earl of Arundel, Lord Windsor and Fulke Greville, Philip wore a sumptuous blue and gold engraved suit of armour. The horses were caparisoned in white and carnation silk and there were brilliant trains of gentlemen and yeomen. Trumpeters trumpeted, gunners in crimson sarcenet shot odoriferous charges of sweet powders and waters, and footmen planted pretty scaling ladders against the Fortress of Perfect Beauty (the Queen's seat, naturally) and threw flowers and 'such fancies'. Meanwhile the hosts, calling themselves the Foster Children of Desire, advanced with ringing verses behind a 'rolling trench' equipped with 'divers kind of most excellent musike', demanding the surrender of the Fortress—and so it continued for two days with more and more expensive trappings. To avoid the New Year present-giving Philip would vanish to Wilton to stay with his sister, the Countess of Pembroke. His death is famous: in pain and nearly fainting from a fatal wound in his thigh, received when fighting against the Netherlands, he heroically keeps his saddle and resigns his cup of water to a dying soldier, then pledges the fellow's health in the dregs. Gossipy old John Aubrey stains the legend by telling us that the real cause of Sir Philip's death was that, against the advice of his surgeons, he would not 'forbeare his carnall knowledge' of his wife, who had hurried out to nurse him. As for his sister, Aubrey tells us, she was very salacious. 'In the Spring of the yeare, when the stallions were to leap the Mares' she would watch them through a *vidette* and then 'act the sport herselfe with *her* stallions', one of whom John Aubrey had heard being none other than her chivalrous brother himself, indeed Aubrey had heard old gentlemen say that Philip, Earl of Pembroke, was begot by him: 'but he inherited not the witt of either brother or sister.'

The gap between courtiers and country bumpkins.

As for their unfortunate parents they had assets that were quite diminished by duties to their Queen. Sir Henry Sidney was obliged to subsidise expeditions from his own pocket and by the end of his life he had spent £30,000 of his estate. His wife contracted smallpox from Elizabeth when nursing her and, while Her Majesty remained unmarked, Lady Mary's face was ruined. Finally in 1572 the Queen did agree to confer a barony on him, but offered no land so that Lady Mary had to write to Lord Burghley asking him to use 'his endeavours that her husband may not be raised to the peerage in consideration of their inability to maintain a higher title than they now possess'. A title was pointless without supporting land since if there were no funds the bearer could not fulfil his aristocratic functions—although a possible solution was to trade one's title and marry an heiress.

The material failure of such loyal subjects as the Sidneys, d'Eresby and Essex did nothing to discourage people from coming to London. In 1593 the court became so crowded that a proclamation was published to restrain the access of so many suitors. Prospective courtiers were greatly assisted by the development of the coach. Hitherto journeys had been major adventures undertaken on horse. Sir John Oglander records that when the gentry of the Isle of Wight went to London '(thinkynge it a East India voyage) they alwaies made thyr willes'. Now people could arrive at their ease. 'There is no reason to leave you where you are at Penshurst without company in the winter,' Sir Robert Sidney wrote off to his wife in 1594. 'London is the garden of

England, whear wee may all live together,' Sir Anthony Denton told Thomas Isham. The delights of this garden included 'rich wives, spruce mistresses, pleasant houses, good dyet, rare wines, neat servants'. There was also Harry Hunks the bear to be baited in the Paris Gardens, a wonderful camel and a curious horse. There were innumerable prostitutes and brothels to frequent and two playhouses to visit—the Globe and Blackfriars—and there were the tombs at Westminster. Compared to all this the country was apparently a dull and lonely place. 'I have not yet been a day in the country and I am as weary of it as I had been prisoner there for 7 years,' the Earl of Pembroke wrote from Wilton in 1601. All through King James's reign increasing numbers of the nobility, echoing his sentiment, were sucked into London.

James I, whose physical appearance was not promising.

Chapter 2

K ING James's court was less polished than Elizabeth's and more
corrupt. The physical appearance of James himself was not
promising. His eyes rolled, his beard was thin, his tongue was too
large for his mouth, his legs were weak, his walk circular and his fingers
forever fiddling in his codpiece.

Where Elizabeth had been parsimonious with her hand-outs James was
promiscuous. During the forty-four years of Elizabeth's reign 878 knights
were created; during the thirty-nine years of the early Stuarts (1603–1641),
3,281. By 1605 James was using honours to reward anyone who took his
fancy. He knighted his goldsmith William Herrick 'for making a hole in the
great diamond the king doth wear'. Furthermore he distributed the right of
nominations among his courtiers which passed like stocks and shares into the
general currency, so that in 1606 Lionel Cranfield could buy the making of
six knights from his friend Arthur Ingram for £373.1.8. Baronetcies and
earldoms were sold to meet pressing needs. In 1616 large sums were required
to launch Sir James Hay on his embassy to Paris and two baronetcies were
sold to Sir John Holles and Sir John Roper. Hay had migrated from Scotland
with James and the move seems to have gone to his head. When he gave a
banquet to the French Ambassador he dished up fish of such size that the
plates had to be made especially. He liked to serve pies stuffed with
ambergris, musk and pearls and he introduced antesuppers at which the
tables were covered with dishes so tall that, when the fashion came to be
generally adopted, most houses had to have their doors enlarged to admit the
dinner. In Paris he had his horses shod with silver shoes, so lightly nailed
that they were perpetually being thrown off. On his return he was given the
creation of two barons as compensation for his outlay and was made a

viscount in return for money which went to buy hangings to furnish houses along the route of the royal journey to Scotland.

At first, efforts were made to prevent the new currency of dignities from inflation. But soon they became commonplace and the royal finances were propped up by the sale of peerages. The making of a baronet was one of the favours granted to certain courtiers to be resold on the market to the highest bidder. In 1622 when the City of Lincoln was trying to raise money to drain and deepen the Foss dyke James granted the city the making of three baronets. By offering over a hundred baronetcies from 1619 to 1622 Buckingham and the King flooded the market, the price fell from £700 to £220. Sir John Oglander records that a seller of baronetcies came peddling his wares round the Isle of Wight and the price was pushed down to £200. Up until 1615 the peerage still retained full dignity, hardly anyone was admitted to the ranks who was unworthy of the honour by birth and wealth. From 1615 there was a change of policy which resulted in inflation of the peerage, a system of direct cash for sales of titles. It was no coincidence that the change of policy coincided with the rise of Buckingham—whose own finances were past praying for, he lived for most of his life from hand to mouth without the faintest idea of the state of his affairs.

Buckingham, 'the handsomest bodied man in England', has also been called the first materialist. In 1616 he enjoyed the decorative honour of being the King's Master of the Horse, next he rose to Baron of Whaddon, then Viscount Villiers, by 1617 he was Earl of Buckingham, 1618 Marquis, 1623 Duke. Egged on by his mother who was a vulgar virago he advanced his own family. He had an almost inexhaustible supply of female relations who were in turn matched with Middlesex, Manchester, the Marquis of Hamilton and so on. His brothers were particular objects of the King's benevolence. John ended insane, but not before becoming Viscount Purbeck and marrying a daughter of Sir Edward Coke with a dowry of £10,000 (although it had not been easy; the girl's mother had refused to consent, obliging lawsuits and a rushed marriage). Buckingham's own marriage had been the cause of some scandal. During his researches he had violated many noble virgins. When finally a match was arranged with Lady Katharine Manners her father, the Duke of Rutland, did not seem to appreciate the great honour: not surprising considering the bridegroom demanded a dowry of £20,000 and lands worth £4,000.

But, for James, Buckingham performed the role of entertainer and whirled away the ennui of court life. Horatio Buscino describes a court masque in 1618. 'Last of all they danced the Spanish dance, one at a time each with his lady, and being well nigh tired they began to lag, whereupon the king who is

George Villiers, 1st Duke of Buckingham:
'the handsomest bodied man in England'.

habitually choleric got impatient, and shouted aloud. "Why don't they dance? What did they make me come here for? Devil take you all, dance." Upon this Buckingham immediately sprang forward, cutting a score of lofty and very minute capers with so much grace and agility that he not only appeased the ire of his angry lord but rendered himself the admiration and delight of everybody.'

By 1621 enormous sums were needed to pay Buckingham's embassy to Paris and a new round of title sales began in order to raise £30,000. Lady Burgh asked for the making of a baron in compensation for the surrender of her pension of £400 which had been granted by Elizabeth. Sir Thomas Garrard asked Buckingham for compensation for the loss of £4,000 he had been paid for a patent in the manufacture of tobacco pipes. Could he, he suggested, be repaid out of the £10,000 he would obtain from a respectable candidate were he to be given the making of a baron? The commonest method of obtaining a peerage was payment to Buckingham or his relations. Robert Pierrepoint said that he was told by the Duke's doctor that he could be a baron for £4,000, a viscount for £4,000 more and an earl for yet another £4,000. By July 1629 he was Earl of Kingston.

All over England the heralds were busy designing new coats of arms. A long pedigree had always been useful to the Tudors. Heralds had been busy contriving vast rolls tracing ancestors back to the Normans, Romans and Trojans. Some were not satisfied until they got back to heroes of the Old Testament. The Popham family tree began with an illustration of Noah sitting in his ark. Lord Lumley removed three mediaeval effigies—which were probably not his ancestors at all—from Durham and exhibited them proudly at Chester-le-Street. He and his relations boasted so loudly of their ancestors that King James is supposed to have remarked: 'I did na ken Adam's name was Lumley.'

Most of King James's courtiers were office seekers, hoping for commissions in the British army and spoils from the prolific sales of titles. Other goodies to be had were the parasitic monopolies attached to trade and industries. Anyone of any consequence at court tried to procure one of these. The building of lighthouses, salting fish, the inspection and measurement of woollen cloth, the collection of debts due to the Crown, all these carried monopolies ripe for the picking. Extravagant Lord Hay enjoyed one on the manufacture of starch—a coup in the age of ruffs and cuffs—while Buckingham's relations, Sir Edward and Christopher Villiers, were enhanced by the retail sale of wine, manufacture of glass, and gold and silver thread.

To live up to their honours the new nobility had to maintain a grand standard of living. Like all good courtiers it was vital to be well-dressed in

Henry, Prince of Wales, who died under suspicious circumstances.

the latest style, to entertain lavishly and to own sumptuous coaches and footmen. Buckingham equipped his carriage with as many as six horses which provoked the Earl of Northumberland—who prided himself on the ancestry in which Buckingham was deficient—into getting eight. Fashions flooded into London: French standing collars, Danish hanging sleeves, galligaskins, blistered codpieces. King James bought a new cloak every month, a waistcoat every three weeks, a suit every ten days, a pair of stockings, boots and garters every four or five days and a new pair of gloves every day. Silks alone cost the King and Queen over £10,000 a year. Men were decked out in figured satins, crimson velvet, ermine brocades, gold and silver. They wore tasselled earrings, immense pleated breeches, carnation silk stockings and coloured feathers from exotic birds. Fantastic lace roses concealed their shoe buckles, incredible ruffs radiated out in wired and starched salients. Ladies pinched, pulled and stuffed themselves into the shapes that elegance demanded. A single dress for Lady Boyle in 1604 required canvas and stuffing to puff out the gown, whalebone to compress the bodice, buckram to support the wings, pasteboard and wire to hold up the collar. In 1614 an angry orator in the House of Commons shouted, 'Women carry manors and thousands of oak trees about their necks.'

Conspicuous consumption is seen by historians to be a cause of family decay second only to biological failure. Major expenses in pomp and circumstance in royal service undid the Earl of Huntingdon. The cost of attendance at court was the ruin of the Windsors and Norths. Speeches on the scaffold before execution were favourite occasions for a display of repentance on a misspent life at court. Sir Walter Ralegh said: 'I have been a soldier, a sailor and a courtier, which are courses of wickedness and vice.' Mrs Turner the poisoner lamented, 'O the Court, the Court! God bless the King and send him better servants about him, for there is no religion in most of them but malice, pride, whoredom, swearing and rejoicing in the fall of others. It is so wicked a place as I wonder the earth did not open and swallow it up.'

Perhaps it was because Elizabeth had been so parsimonious that there was so little corruption in her court. There had been gossip certainly and the occasional misdemeanour, but nothing compared to the goings-on at James's court. First there was the betting. In a single day Lord Howard de Walden lost over £1,500 betting at bowls. Wagers were placed on races between running footmen. In 1618 there was a race between an English footman belonging to the Countess of Bedford and an Irishman serving the Earl of Suffolk. When the race was over Buckingham collected £3,000 from those who had backed the Irishman.

Robert Carr, Earl of Somerset.

Then there were the scandals, as a result of which sexual licence became associated with the aristocracy. Southampton, Pembroke and Sir Walter Ralegh all got Maids of Honour pregnant. The King of Denmark accused the Countess of Northampton of being a whore and, according to Lady Anne Clifford, 'all the ladies about the court had gotten such ill names that it was grown a scandalous place'. Next, Lady Ross publicly accused her husband of impotence, then charged the Countess of Exeter with 'adultery, incest, murther, poison and suchlike peccadilos': the affair ended with Lady Ross's accusations being exposed as lies and herself being convicted of incest with her brother.

Most scandalous of all affairs had been early on in the reign (when James's favourite had been Somerset) and involved Lady Essex. She had married the son of Elizabeth's ill-fated favourite when they were children. He had travelled, as was the standard, and she remained at court and, according to gossip, engaged in profligacy. Prince Henry had enjoyed her favours, it seems, and Somerset was madly in love, wanting to marry her. Poor Prince Henry had died under suspicious circumstances (Somerset being suspected of poisoning him) and everyone had been astonished at supper by a handsome young man dashing naked into St James's, saying he was the prince's ghost come down from heaven with a message from the King. Then the Earl of Essex was accused of impotence and a divorce arranged. Sir Thomas Ovebury, who was against the suit, was imprisoned in the Tower and a few days later died poisoned by jelly. Lady Essex and Somerset enjoyed a grand marriage, but their bliss was short-lived, they were both arrested and sent to the Tower. They managed to blackmail their way out but died poor and miserable—she, according to gossip, of venereal disease.

Divorce, promiscuity and poison were not enough. Many of the court masques were anything but ideal and developed into orgies of astonishing dissipation. The Queen gave a pageant and spent the evening sitting in a large scallop shell with, among others, the Ladies Bedford, Suffolk and Rich, all of them with their faces and their arms painted black. The night was supposed to have concluded with a banquet but it was so furiously assaulted that the table collapsed before one mouthful could be eaten.

The most famous occasion of all was at Theobalds in 1606 when for five days Burleigh entertained King James and the King of Denmark at a cost of £1,180. 'I ne'er did see such lack of good order, discretion and sobriety as I have now done,' remarked Sir John Harington, and continued that he had been well nigh overwhelmed with carousal and sports of all kinds. 'We had women . . . of such plenty, as would have astonished each beholder. Our feasts were magnificent and the two royal guests did most lovingly embrace each other.' As for the courtiers, they, as usual, were supposed to be acting an allegory, the Coming of the Queen of Sheba before Solomon, a performance designed to flatter the King of Denmark who was supposed to represent wisdom in the act of receiving great wealth. Unfortunately the actors were so drunk that they either fell down or were sick. The lady playing the Queen's part tripped up the steps to the canopy sheltering Their Majesties and upset all the caskets of precious gifts into his Danish Majesty's face. After much confusion and mopping up His Majesty rose and would dance with the Queen of Sheba, but he fell down as well and had to be carried off to an inner chamber, 'not a little defiled with the presents which had been bestowed on his garments: such as wine, cream, jelly, cakes, spices and other good matters'. The show went forward but most of the actors went backwards or fell down. 'Then appeared, in rich dresses, Hope, Faith and Charity. Hope tried to speak, but wine so enfeebled her endeavours that she withdrew and hoped the king would excuse her brevity. Faith followed her from the Royal presence in a staggering condition. Charity came to the king's feet and, seeming desirous to cover the sins of her sisters, made a sort of obeisance, she brought gifts, but said she would return home again, as there

Most scandalous of all affairs: Somerset and his bride, Lady Essex.

was no gift which heaven had not already given His Majesty: she then returned to Hope and Faith, who were both sick in the lower hall . . .' The ceremonies concluded by Peace hitting some courtiers on the head with an olive branch. On a similar occasion a courtier was discovered dead on the dinner table with wine foaming out of his mouth: 'a horrid sight to behold.'

One of the causes underlying the Civil War was loss of confidence in the aristocracy. The House of Commons came to look on the court, and in consequence most of the aristocracy, as a parasitic order preying on the country. The Privy Council and officers of the household disapproved strongly of the aristocratic migration to London. It was dissipating to health and fortunes, a ready way to decay men and families. Yet each royal return to Westminster saw more of the nobility coming up from the country. The Council reiterated that the right place for a nobleman was in the country serving usefully as a Justice of the Peace and maintaining his house. The nobleman's *duty* was to live in the country and not indulge himself selfishly in London pleasures, while residing in a house which was supported by rents from the country. This was an issue which caused real feeling and was the cause of much aristocratic guilt and ambivalence.* The tradition of country hospitality was being abandoned and family establishments broken up while the city was crowded with idlers. In one petition the writer asks His Majesty 'to cleanse this citie of the superfluous number of idle drones and gaudie butterflies that swarm in and about.'

In 1622 a proclamation commanded: 'Noblemen, knights and gentlemen of quality to repayre to their Mansion houses in the country, and keepe hospitality, according to the ancient and laudable custome of England.' One measure conceived by Charles I to make life unpleasant for country gentlemen, so that they would return home and manage their estates, was to forbid London inns to serve game.

There was little during Charles I's reign to restore people's faith in either

---

*A description exists of an uncouth fellow called Mr Hastings, who was the epitome of a country bumpkin. He lived in 1638 in a house in a large park filled with fishponds, deer, rabbits, a ridged bowling green—it never having been levelled after the plough—and a banqueting house built in a tree. His table was stocked with beef pudding and beer and his hall with marrowbones, hawks, perches, hounds, spaniels and terriers. The upper side was hung with fox-skins and polecats. Terriers and the choicest hounds lay in the parlour. His chair held litters of young cats and three or four always attended him at dinner where he kept a little white stick fourteen inches long lying by his plate with which to defend his meat. At the lower end of the hall was an oyster table, which was in constant use twice a day, all the year round. At the upper end two small tables stood covered in hawks, hoods, bells and two or three green hats holding clutches of pheasant eggs. Next door was the old chapel, the pulpit of which never wanted a cold chine of beef, a venison pasty, a gammon of bacon or a huge apple pie. Mr Hastings seduced all the neighbours' wives and lived to be a hundred.

Jacobean courtiers at the dinner table.

the monarch or the nobility. Women patched their faces with spots of scented Spanish leather cut into crescent moons, stars, diamonds, and coaches and horses. At dinner, dwarfs jumped out of pies; terriers, hares, foxes, frogs and birds all wriggled, hopped and flew out of various gilded dishes. Fools leapt over guests' heads into Quaking Custards, and Lady Purbeck was accused of witchcraft and adultery and made to do penance in a white sheet. On top of it all, the King, outraged by what he took to be continual inroads on the Crown's authority, frustrated by inadequate revenues and failure of numerous proposals for new taxes, dissolved parliament and ruled, himself, for eleven years.

The consequence was civil war, which had much the same effect on the country that the First and Second World Wars were to have in the present century. Customs and beliefs vanished. Nothing was quite the same again. One of the reasons that Charles lost the war was that the aristocracy no longer knew how to fight. They had grown soft with fleshpots and had lost their nerve.

Chapter 3

CHARLES II was restored to the throne in 1660. The coronation was a scene of great rejoicing. People drank the King's health over and over again, the streets were full of vomiting men and women, and Pepys, who had somehow ended up in the royal wine cellar, had never been 'so foxed', and was sick in his host's bed.

Having spent his years of exile in France, the King had adopted certain French attitudes. He could not bear ennui. Everything must be geared to diversion. He surrounded himself with witty debauched young men and soon virtuous members of the aristocracy were seen only on state occasions. The courtiers drank, swore, gambled, made love and frequented masquerades and the play. 'To give a further character,' Anthony Wood wrote, 'though they were neat and gay in their apparell, yet they were very nasty and beastly leaving at their departure their excrements in every corner, in chimneys, studies, cole houses, cellars, rude, rough, whoremongers, vaine, empty, careless.'

There is a famous occasion at the court ball held on the last night of 1662; when the time came for country dances the King called out for the first dance, which he said was 'Cuckolds all awry!'—the old dance of England. With this immortal phrase, Arthur Bryant says, 'the king epitomised his court'. Manners were free and easy, conversation was licentious and the King kissed and toyed openly with any woman he fancied. Matters were not improved by the number of dogs he liked to have round him, accompanying him to Council meetings, sitting in his coach and lying in his bedchamber, where they whelped and suckled their young.

The King's male companions had to be skilled in all kinds of modish vice like winning the favours of mistresses and subterranean figures like the

Charles II, who could not bear ennui.

George Villiers, 2nd Duke
of Buckingham: his appetite
for pleasure was said to be crazy.

King's pimp. The 2nd Duke of Buckingham who, according to his enemies, *was* the King's pimp, had an appetite for pleasure that was said to be crazy. Perpetual surfeits had filled his mind with vicious humours and his body with a nursery of diseases. Continual wine, women and music had given him false values so that he retained no right notions. Certainly he was as extravagant as his father had been and appeared at the coronation in clothes and ornaments supposed to be worth £30,000. By paying £20,000 he achieved the position of the King's Master of the Horse. He was a great tease and mimic and would walk behind the Chancellor, Clarendon, whom everyone hated, with a pair of tongs imitating his gait. Like most courtiers he kept his wife in the country and his mistresses in town—women found him irresistible and his bastards were plentiful. He fought a duel for Lady Shrewsbury and killed her husband, and poor Madame Cozens who slept with him to pay back her husband (who had gone to bed with a chambermaid) ended up ruined and keeping a brothel in the Strand.

As for the 2nd Earl of Rochester, even his parentage was questionable. 'I have been creditably informed by knowing men,' says Anthony Wood, 'that

The Earl of Rochester: even his parentage was questionable.

Anne Hyde, secretly married to 'dismal Jimmy'—the Duke of York.

this John, Earl of Rochester was begotten by Sir Allen Apsley.' At first he charmed everyone with his wit, beauty and learning, but gradually he drank more and more and alienated everyone with his lampoons. One with which he honoured His Majesty went:

Restless he rolls about from whore to whore
A merry monarch scandalous and poor
Nor are his high desires above his strength
His sceptre and his . . . are of a length.

Bishop Burnet claimed that Rochester employed a footman to stand every night outside the doors of ladies he believed to be enjoying intrigues. Then he would retire to the country and write libels. He grew wilder and wilder, going about the streets as a beggar, posing as Dr. Bembo the clairvoyant, pushing people into the Thames, tossing fiddlers in blankets and going round in groups of drunk lords committing acts of vandalism. Once, disguised as a tinker, he collected all the pots and pans from the housewives of Burford and broke instead of mending them (for this he was put into the stocks and had to be rescued by his servants who only got him home by transporting the stocks as well). Another time he and Buckingham, both out of favour at court, fetched up at an inn near Newmarket where one legend has it they dispensed such generous hospitality that all the husbands of the parish got drunk, while Rochester and Buckingham seduced their wives, causing at least one husband to hang himself. Rochester was often committed to the Tower, which Charles used as a sort of inebriates' home, but he would let out again whenever the King needed a good laugh. He died, aged thirty-one, of venereal disease.

But it was the King's brother and heir, the Duke of York (whom everyone hated and was called by Nell Gwynn 'Dismal Jimmy'), who caused him most trouble. He became a Roman Catholic and filled the galleries with his affairs—his mistresses were so plain that Charles said they must have been given to him by his priest for penance. There was a great scandal when he secretly married the Chancellor's daughter, Anne Hyde, and several gallants came forward with stories to blacken her character. The Earl of Arran said he had unlaced her dress while his sister-in-law was playing at ninepins. Thomas Killigrew said he had had the honour of being on the most intimate terms with her in a water closet, that three or four swains had witnessed his happiness and had in all probability witnessed the happiness of several others as well, since the lady frequently repaired to the place and was particularly delighted with it. Some people thought that the Chancellor had especially arranged a barren marriage for the King so that the line of succession should run (as it did) through his own daughter. Everyone knew when the Duke of York had an affair with Lady Carnegie, 'who had already been in several other hands'. It ran through the galleries that her husband had retired in revenge to a noted bawdy house, and procured the foulest whore eaten up with the pox, and having contracted that had given it to Lady Carnegie, who gave it to the Duke of York who had much ado to save his nose and gave it to the Duchess, producing as a result very sickly children.

The King's own morals were not assisted by his Portuguese bride, who was rather ugly and childish—'a very little plain old woman', Pepys called her—with a retinue that was no better, consisting, according to the Chevalier de Grammont, of six frights who called themselves Maids of Honour. For sheer quantity, Charles's mistresses and bastards are renowned. When a Lord Mayor described Charles as 'the father of his people', Buckingham added, 'of a good many of them'. Someone else described him as the 'known enemy to virginity and chastity'. He had fourteen acknowledged bastards, including the Dukes of St Albans, Southampton, Richmond, Grafton, Northumberland and Monmouth. During his exile it was rumoured that Lady Byron was his seventeenth whore (she was very avaricious and would not leave him until he had given an order for £4,000 worth of plate to be made for her; she died before she could get it, but not before extracting £15,000 from Charles during his exile and on his restoration securing a pension of £500 a year).

To be one of Charles's mistresses was not a position of dignity. Most invoked the derision of Pepys and his friends who called them harlots, whores, jades, sluts and the like. Pepys, however, loved Lady Castlemaine. She was a lascivious beauty, with auburn hair, blue almond-shaped eyes, vital, wanton, extravagant and deceitful. At first the King was infatuated with her and would dine at her lodgings—above one of the gatehouses—four or five times a week, sneaking back to the palace early in the morning. Their quarrels and reconciliations constituted the chief news of the court. When she was cross she screamed like a fishwife, no matter who was there. Even her petticoats were available for viewing in the Privy Gardens: 'saw the finest smocks and linen petticoats of My Lady Castlemayne,' records Pepys, 'laced with rich lace at the bottomes that ever I saw and did me good to look upon them.' Nearly every year she 'slipped a filly'. Five of her children were acknowledged by the King: Anne, who married the Earl of Sussex, Charles, Duke of Southampton, Henry, Duke of Grafton, Charlotte, who married the Earl of Lichfield, and George, Duke of Northumberland. She did not have an easy time. People would accost her in the street suggesting that she would end up like Jane Shore, the mistress of Edward IV, who died in poverty and was dumped on a manure heap. She was too clever for such a fate however

Lady Castlemaine, who screamed like a fishwife.

Nell Gwynn, a dangerous rival.

and materially did well from the liaison. She received Irish property with her title, in addition to which she collected £6,000 a year from excise, £3,000 for each of her children and £4,700 from the Post Office. She was supposed to be so randy that when her affair with the King was over, and she was pensioned off as the Duchess of Cleveland, she kept salaried lovers—she also favoured John Churchill, the future Duke of Marlborough, starting him up the ladder of success.

Charles was fonder of Nell Gwynn than all his other mistresses. She did not meddle in public affairs, she was not avaricious and she was very funny. She was given a property on the south side of Pall Mall, with a garden bordering St James's Park, and conceived two royal bastards. She never pestered the King for titles and there are various stories about the creation of the Duke of St Albans. One is that the King was riding by one day when Nell was in a rage and threatened to throw her son out of the window. With great presence of mind, the King called out: 'Save the Duke of St Albans.' Her youngest son, James Beauclerc, died in France in 1680.

Nell was a dangerous rival. Moll Davis, another actress, became the King's mistress in 1668. She was seen at the theatre by Pepys, the King gazing on her 'even to the scorn of the whole world'. Poor Lady Castlemaine, who went wherever the King went, was out of humour all the play, not smiling once, while Moll 'the most impertinent slut in the world', and a bastard of Lord Berkshire's besides, displayed a ring, telling everybody that it had cost £700 and that the King had given it to her. 'And he hath furnished a house for her in Suffolk Street most richly . . . which is most infinite shame.' She gave birth to a daughter, Mary Tudor, who was acknowledged by the King, but Nell Gwynn was her undoing. On hearing that the King was planning a horizontal rendezvous, gossip has it that she entertained Moll beforehand to a collation of sweetmeats, laced with laxatives. A violent and sudden looseness wrecked the bed and assaulted the lovers, and Moll was sacked, with a pension of £1,000 per annum, and never appeared at court again.

Nell hated Lady Castlemaine's successor, Louise de Kérouaille, who was promoted to Duchess of Portsmouth. She called her 'Weeping Willow' and 'Squintabella', made faces behind her back and jokes at her expense. During one fight she is supposed to have whipped up Her Grace's coats and burnt off her pubic hair with a candle. When the Duchess complained to the King, Nell said that since parliament had recently passed an act forbidding importation of foreign commodities that prejudiced the growth of English trade she had merely been burning prohibited goods. In spite of this the Duchess managed to conceive two children, Louise, who became a nun, and Charles, the Duke of Richmond.

The King's restoration had drawn a number of foreigners to the court. Into England flowed an increasing stream of French ideas, silver tooth-brushes, sedan chairs, fans, petticoats, gold sealing wax and gilt mirrors. Everything French was fashionable except for the French themselves. Those that appeared at court were a disgrace—mostly insignificant young puppies, each

The Chevalier de Grammont, the court gossip.

trying to outdo the other in extravagance. The Chevalier de Grammont, however, was something other. Exiled from France, where he had apparently killed his wife by locking her into a chamber of which the floor gave way, precipitating her into a deep pit, he was familiar with everyone and their intrigues.

Beauties were everywhere, he said, of the court. Lady Castlemaine, Lady Chesterfield, Lady Shrewsbury and a hundred others, but Miss Hamilton and Miss Stewart were the main ornaments. Love was the chief pursuit. Spies were posted at doors, letters flew about, looking-glasses, scented gloves, apricot paste and essences were dispatched from Paris and jewels hurried round from City jewellers. But, most of all, everyone busied himself in amusing the King. The Chevalier de Grammont provided delicious collations and musical entertainments conveyed from Paris. Lady Castlemaine used all her ingenuity. Her cleverness in keeping her influence over the King was noticeable in the case of Frances Stuart. Charles was besotted by her, openly kissing and cuddling her—although her virtue was said to be king-proof. Lady Castlemaine made her her favourite and invited her to all her parties. With the greatest indiscretion she even kept her there to sleep, it was said, and the King who liked to visit her before she dressed in the morning seldom failed to find Miss Stewart in bed with her. Pepys and his friends shook their heads over their morning draughts. It reached their ears that there had been a frolic between Lady Castlemaine and Miss Stewart. They would be married and married they were, with ring and all the ceremonies of church service, ribbands, sack posset and flinging the stocking.

In fine weather and especially on May Day the fashionable thing was to repair to Hyde Park. Pepys was fond of going there to have a look at the beauties and their naked necks. Often he and everybody else was disappointed by the horrid dust, which was so common that there is a poem: 'And then to Hide-Park do repair, To make a dust and take no air.' One year everyone flocked there to see Lady Newcastle, but the coach was so 'fallowed and crowded upon', without pleasure or order, that they could see only its black and white curtains and the lady's cap. The Chevalier had overheard some ladies complaining that the windows of their coaches did not display them to full advantage. So he had a wonderful glass coach brought over from Paris. Miss Stewart and Lady Castlemaine, who was pregnant at the time, quarrelled over who should ride first in the equipage. Lady Castlemaine said she would miscarry if Miss Stewart was first and Miss Stewart said she would never get pregnant at all if her request were not granted; the Queen, who desired the King to let *her* appear in it first with the Duchess of York, was quite ignored and it was Miss Stewart who won. The poor Queen longed to please the King. It seems she was the only woman of his acquaintance incapable of giving him a child. Instead she gave splendid parties—which were more occasions for Miss Hamilton and Buckingham to play practical jokes than anything else. Lady Muskerry was one of their victims, a rich, ugly heiress, with two short legs, one shorter than the other. She loved dancing and never missed a ball at court—much to the disapproval of her husband who could bear nothing ridiculous and certainly not the spectacle of his wife capering about. When she was six or seven months pregnant she had danced at one of the Queen's fêtes. Her appearance had been worse than ever because the child had fallen all on one side and, to achieve symmetry, she had pinned a cushion inside her dress. Cavorting with uncommon briskness, in case Lord Muskerry should appear before she had fully satisfied herself, the cushion came adrift and fell to the ground. Buckingham

Frances Stewart, said to be King-proof.

took it up instantly and wrapping it in his coat mimicked the cries of a new-born infant as he went round inquiring among the Maids of Honour for a nurse.

Again the Queen contrived a masquerade, those she appointed to dance had to represent different nations. It was to be such a magnificent affair that it would be impossible for Lady Muskerry to take part. Nevertheless Lord Muskerry gave his wife a good talking to, advising her very seriously to content herself with watching, and forbidding her absolutely to dance. Lady Muskerry was furious. But then she received a note from Miss Hamilton, dispatched in exactly the same manner as the Queen's billet, directing her to be dressed for the masquerade in Babylonian fashion. Delighted, she rushed off to discover from merchants who traded in the Levant how ladies of quality dressed in Babylon. Next she proceeded to Miss Hamilton to complain that Lord Muskerry (who before their marriage could have passed whole days and nights in seeing her dance) now thought it proper to forbid her to dance at all. And if Miss Hamilton knew what a plague it was to discover, in that cursed city, how the people of Babylon dressed, she would pity her—and as for the cost . . .

On the great night the Chevalier, whose own apparel had apparently sunk in a quicksand somewhere near Calais, and who was having to appear in ordinary court dress, had his ill-humour increased as he was getting out of his chair by 'the devil of a phantom in masquerade'—she must have had, said he, sixty ells of gauze and silver tissue about her, not to mention a sort of pyramid on her head adorned with a hundred thousand baubles. Lord Muskerry stopped to hear no more. His worst fears were realised. There was Lady Muskerry a thousand times more ridiculous than she had ever been before. He had appalling difficulty in getting her home and had to place a sentry outside her door.

The court was a spectacle for many besides the actual courtiers. Whitehall was almost a public promenade. What with the music, the glowing fabrics and tapestries and the streams of people flowing in by boat and coach, one country squire remarked it was like a fair all day. The galleries were filled with subjects wandering about freely, looking at the court celebrities, relishing the gossip and watching the King and Queen dine in the perfumed Banqueting Hall. Pepys would go there during the Season two or three times a week, drink a morning draught in one of the taverns, then go to the Privy Seal and on to the Wardrobe to dine with Lady Sandwich. The scandals would provide topics of conversation for days afterwards. His main purveyor of news was James Pearse, surgeon to the Duke of York and Groom of the Bedchamber to the Queen, who was able to tell him 'all the businesses of the court, the amours and mad doings that were there'.

'Enjoyed a good discourse with Mr Pearse,' Pepys would write: Lady Castlemaine's latest amour was Jacob Hall the rope dancer; two of the Queen Mother's servants had raped a woman as she was lying in bed with her husband and abused her with a lighted torch; a child had been dropped at a court ball and nobody knew whose since it had been taken up by somebody in their handkerchief; the King had been drunk; he had taken the part of Sir Charles Sedley and Lord Charles Buckhurst who had been running up and down the streets all night with bare arses and were clapped in jail; Sir Charles Sedley had appeared naked again on the balcony of a cook house in Covent Garden and acted all the postures of lust and buggery that could be imagined and 'from thence', Pepys writes, 'preaching a Mountebanke sermon from that pulpitt, saying that there he hath to sell such a pouder as should make all cunts in town run after him—a thousand people standing underneath to see and hear him. And that being done he took a glass of wine and washed his prick in it and then drank it off.'

Again and again Pepys complains of the viciousness of the court and the contempt the King brought himself into: 'so they are all mad and this is how the kingdom is governed,' he writes on one occasion, and on another: 'Hebden did today in the coach tell me how he is vexed to see things at court ordered as they are; by nobody that attends business, but every man himself or his pleasures.'

The gap between town and country widened more than ever. As Killigrew said, a girl educated at court was a terrible piece of furniture for the country. The King and his court were isolated and out of touch with the nation. The unfashionable and poor either hated or envied the frivolity, luxury, immorality and ostentation, while the courtier had a scornful idea of the country. A young person's gibbet and galleys was what de Grammont called the place. Comedies of the period are full of country knights and their wives arriving in London wearing uncouth garments and having frightful manners. 'I wish you were married and living in the country,' Rochester is supposed to have said to a dog that had bitten him, it was the nastiest thing he could think of. The unfashionable squires and reformers called themselves Whigs and formed an opposition, claiming to represent the nation at large against that small corrupt faction—the court and its creatures.

Buckingham entertaining the King to an orgy.

Louis XIV.

Chapter 4

ALTHOUGH Charles II's court was directly influenced by that of Louis XIV, the two were quite different. Charles would kiss and fondle any lady that took his fancy in front of everyone and, although he was a kind man, he was often sullen with his Queen and exposed her to every gossiping tongue, while the vices of his courtiers were the talk of the town. The French court was dignified and bound with etiquette to the point of tedium. Louis XIV behaved with complete respect to his Queen (who had a pretty face, short legs and black teeth, knew very well how to behave but had the mentality of a child and loved playing with little dogs and half-mad dwarfs). He habitually slept in her bed and made love to her at least twice a month—everybody knew when that happened because she went to Communion next day. She would wink her eyes and rub her hands together. She was, Nancy Mitford says, very unattractive.

Versailles had a purpose. It was a magnificent cage in which Louis could keep his aristocracy. Cunningly, he used the French love of fashion and pleasure and gathered everyone under one roof, exercising them with ceremony, keeping them busy all day long running from one end of the palace to the other. It worked. The heaviest blow that could befall a man was banishment to his estates, where he was considered a ridiculous exile.

Louis loved splendour. He liked to see indulgence in entertainments, equipages, building and gambling. In the view of Saint-Simon he put a premium on luxury because he wanted to see everyone ruined. Saint-Simon saw a calculated policy aimed at reduction of the nobility. Taine has a famous passage where he likens the court to a flask of gold and crystal: to fill it with scent a great nobility must be made barren of fruit and bear only flowers.

With their owners cooped up in a perpetual house-party, estates were neglected and milked of their crops and timber. 'I have been ready to weep to see the desolated condition of this estate,' Madame de Sévigné writes on one of her rare trips to Brittany. 'There were the finest trees in the world upon it, and my son in his last journey gave the finishing stroke to the last of them. He would even have sold a little copse, which was the greatest ornament of the place . . . He scraped together 400 pistoles by this plunder, of which he had not a single penny left in a month's time . . . he is a perpetual drain, and what he does with his money I cannot perceive: for my part I believe his hand is a crucible which melts the money the instant it is put into it.' Rural France became like a desert overrun by stags, wild boars, wolves and the hunt itself, while the Ile de France was like an enormous park containing thousands of glorious houses.

No one has constructed the life at Versailles better than Nancy Mitford. The palace was like Aladdin's cave, glittering with new gilding, lit by thousands of candles in silver chandeliers, furnished with solid silver consoles, tables of porphyry and alabaster, silver tubs of orange trees, damask curtains embroidered with gold, and beautiful women shining in satin and lace, embroidered, re-embroidered and over-embroidered with gold thread and covered with jewels. Hundreds of nobles were crammed into the north wing, which was penetrated by a maze of corridors where strangers lost themselves. Some apartments were merely rooms chopped into tiny units, some had no windows or gave into dismal interior wells. However squalid a lodging might be, it was a sign of having succeeded in life. Like their English counterparts the poorer members of the nobility could easily find themselves ruined by the life and the clothes. When people felt they could no longer meet the expenses they would hope for presents from the King—cash, or a lucrative sinecure usually acquired through his mistresses, who took a percentage.

Unlike the English, the French aristocracy were still warriors. As soon as the winter was over, all able-bodied men rode off to the front. The court itself was run with military precision, a rigid etiquette was necessary for controlling a population of between two and five thousand. Great nobles lived tied down by daily ceremonies, the King's *lever* and *coucher*, his *débotter* (when he changed after hunting), his dinner, eaten in public, and his procession to chapel. Louis was God. His particular look through half-shut eyes was bestowed every day on hundreds of people. Absentees were noticed at once. It was unwise to play truant. Permission to leave might be granted for those wanting to visit their estates, but not for a frivolous outing

Versailles, a magnificent cage.

to Paris. In order to keep everyone at home there was a constant stream of entertainments. Events in the King's own family, like births, marriages and deaths, rated highly as diversion. Madame Duchess of Orleans, who was married to the King's brother, Monsieur, wrote that she was to attend the christening of all three of the Dauphin's sons. 'I am to hold the Duc de Bourgogne with the King. A great many diamonds are being prepared for our adornment but with my cold I shall probably look like a shat-on carrot (by your leave, by your leave).'

'I was on Saturday at Versailles,' wrote Madame de Sévigné in 1676. 'You know the ceremony of attending the Queen at her toilette, at mass, and at dinner, but there is now no necessity of being stifled with the heat and with the crowd.' When their majesties had dined, the King, the Queen, Monsieur, Madame, Mademoiselle, all the Princes and Princesses, Madame de Montespan and all her train, all the courtiers and all the ladies—in a word the whole court of France—retired to that fine apartment of the King's which was furnished with the utmost magnificence. There one did not know what it was to be incommoded with heat, one could pass from one place to another without being in the least crowded. Music played of a soft and delicate kind and the magnificence of the court was beyond imagination.

Every Monday, Wednesday and Friday there was the *jour d'appartement*. All the gentlemen would assemble in the King's antechamber, while the women met in the Queen's rooms at six o'clock. Everyone went in procession to the drawing room. Next door was a large room where fiddles played for those who wanted to dance. Through this was the King's throne room where every kind of music was played and sung. Then came the bedchamber with three card tables, one for the King, one for the Queen and one for Monsieur, a large room with twenty tables covered in green velvet with gold fringes for more games, and a long room with refreshments adjoining another with four more tables just as long laden with decanters and glasses and every kind of wine and liqueur. Those who did not play wandered from room to room, now to the music, now to the gamblers.

There were two sorts of nobility at Versailles: *noblesse de race*, which was the old feudal aristocracy, and *noblesse de robe*, obtained through office. Rules surrounding the ordinary procedure of everyday life were such that before Madame d'Etoiles (the future Madame de Pompadour) could be presented at court she had to go away for several months and have lessons. There was for example a special salute for every woman at court according to her own and her husband's birth—the quality of her housekeeping and her suppers all came into it. A movement of the shoulder which practically amounted to an insult was a suitable greeting for a woman of moderate birth who was badly married with a poor cook, while a well-born duchess received a deep obeisance. The most ordinary movements and expressions were studied as though on stage. There was a particular way of sitting down and getting up, of holding the knife, fork and glass, and of walking. You could tell a court lady from a Parisian by her walk—a sort of gliding run with very fast tiny steps so that you looked like a mechanical doll with wheels. Cheerfulness was good manners—and you got nowhere at Versailles without good manners— therefore the look and general demeanour must be happy. The usher opening

Madame de Sévigné.
OVERLEAF: A *divertissement* at Versailles.

a door would stand inside it when certain people passed through and outside it for others. Then there was *le pour*. When writing place-cards or labels of reservation, *pour le Duc de X* ranked higher in esteem than *le Duc de X*. People would do anything to get the *pour*. The Princesse des Ursins when visiting Marly fainted with joy when she discovered *pour Mme des Ursins* on her door panel and had to be given salts. Occupants of a sedan chair must stop and get out when meeting a member of the royal family while the occupants of a carriage must stop the horse and not get out. Dukes were allowed to take a *carré*—the word *coussin* was taboo—to sit or kneel on in chapel, but they must put it down crooked, only Princes of the Blood might have it straight. The only people ever allowed to sit in an armchair when the King was present were his wives, the King of England and the King's grandson when he became King of Spain. But although etiquette was rigid and everyone was polite to a degree—or anyway when they were in public—there was nothing priggish about them. 'I can't resist telling you of a splendid conversation I had with Monsieur,' wrote Madame. 'I hope it will amuse you as much as it did my two children. There were just the four of us in my apartments after supper: Monsieur, me, my son and my daughter. Monsieur, who didn't consider us fine enough company to trouble himself by talking, after a long silence let off a great long fart (by your leave, by your leave). He turned to me and said, "What was that, Madame?" I turned my behind in his direction, let off in the same tone and said, "That, Monsieur." My son said, "If it comes to that, I can do as well as Monsieur and Madame," and let off a good one, too. Then we all laughed and left the room . . .'

Being a mistress of Louis XIV was altogether a grander affair than being one of Charles II's ladies. Immediately after the death of his mother Anne of Austria, Louis recognised Louise de la Vallière as his titular mistress. But she was, as Nancy Mitford says, a woman to be hidden away and visited by moonlight, in the role of declared mistress she was inadequate. She sat next to Louis at the *Divertissement* he gave as a sort of house-cooling party to the old establishment. She was pregnant, dull and melancholy and the King's attention was taken by another table where the Marquise de Montespan and her friend Mlle Scarron (the future Madame de Maintenon) were sparkling.

No one could have been cleverer or more amusing than Madame de Montespan. She had inherited an irresistible way of talking—lazy, languid, wailing, building up an episode with exaggeration and comic images until everyone was rolling about with laughter. She had the ability to make other people shine. At first the King would not look at her and she resorted to the fashionable fortune-teller Madame Voisin, who catered for such desires as larger breasts, smaller mouths, whiter hands and so on. She was well versed

Madame de Montespan with her children.

in spells for unrequited love, and knew a priest who read the gospel over Madame de Montespan's head and prepared a nostrum of pigeon's hearts under a chalice. And lo! The King went off to besiege Lille taking Madame de Montespan as lady-in-waiting to the Queen. Monsieur de Montespan was furious, he boxed his wife's ears, talked loudly about David and Bathsheba and drove about with a pair of horns on the roof of his coach. Then he went into mourning and referred to his late wife. It made no difference. In 1673 the King went again to the front with Madame de Montespan, who was now heavily pregnant, Louise de la Vallière and the Queen, all lumbering after the army in the same coach. Then he built a house for her at Clagny, which was neither large nor grand enough to please her, so it was pulled down and a more suitably scaled château was designed by Mansart. Her brother was made Captain General of the Galleys, her father Governor of Paris, and her niece was married to the Duc de Nevers, who according to Madame de Sévigné always had his hands in unexpected places.

When the King travelled it was only with women, his theory being that if he spent several hours alone with a man he would be sure to ask some favour. The journeys were a nightmare, in the coldest weather the windows must be open, and his companions were expected to eat a great deal—he hated people to refuse food—yet on no account must they leave the coach for physical needs. One of his closest friends, the Duchesse of Chevreuse, went alone with him from Versailles to Fontainebleau. Hardly had they left Versailles than she needed to relieve herself. Halfway the King stopped the coach and a meal was served. She consumed as little as she possibly could but her condition worsened. On reaching the destination at last she managed to stagger to the chapel on the arm of her brother-in-law who, on hearing her predicament, hurried her in and mounted guard until she had finished.

The King himself had a huge appetite. At his autopsy it was discovered that his stomach and bowels were twice the usual size and length. Madame said that she had seen him eat four platefuls of different soup, a whole pheasant, a whole partridge, a plateful of salad, mutton hashed with garlic, two good slices of ham, a dish of pastry and afterwards fruit and sweetmeats.

He was always promiscuous and if Madame de Montespan kept him waiting he would go to bed with any woman who was handy. Indeed he had done so in her own ante-chamber with her maid Mlle des Oeillets and with her sister-in-law Mme de Thianges, who regarded herself as one of nature's masterpieces. This was all in the family so to speak and the public knew nothing about it. Suddenly to the consternation of Mesdames de Montespan and Maintenon he turned to a variety of other ladies. The Princesse de Soubise, who was in love with her husband and longing to be of use to him,

'Old Kunkunel', Madame de Maintenon.

dispatched him to his estates and put on her emerald earrings—a signal that the coast was clear. The result was that the Soubises became enormously rich. Then Madame de Fontanges, one of Madame's ladies-in-waiting, 'a stupid little thing but as lovely as an angel', was declared a duchess and began going to Mass in a dress made from the same stuff as the King's coat—everyone knew what *that* meant.

After the birth of the Comte de Toulouse, Madame de Montespan lost her power over the King. She grew fat and used too much scent. She was so helpful in holding his court and such a part of court life he would probably have overlooked this but for her appalling tempers. People talked instead of Madame de Mainten*ant*. She was a religious lady and under her influence the King decided to abandon his promiscuity and devote himself to the Queen—who died soon afterwards. Then, it is thought, he married Madame de Maintenon.

Madame detested Madame de Maintenon and wrote numerous letters calling her an old whore, an old hag, old Kunkunel, Rumpumpel and so on—which were opened and read by the King and Madame de Maintenon. 'As long as the old whore is active things will go badly for me at Court; she detests me,' Madame wrote, and complained that she made the court so tedious it could hardly be endured. 'The King's old drab has ordered all the ladies who use rouge not to do so any longer.' 'It is a miserable thing when people may no longer follow their own communion but have to conform to the whims of whores.' According to her, 'old Kunkunel' had bribed her son to make a bad marriage—to Mlle de Blois, daughter of the King and Madame de Montespan, to whom she referred as a mouse-dropping. As for her daughter, the Dauphin, it seemed, had intended to make an offer, but along had come that old witch and put a stop to it. Her daughter in the end married the Duc de Lorraine with whom apparently she enjoyed a delicious time. 'One hears such strange reports of our son-in-law,' wrote Madame. 'Apparently once, when he was taking a bath, the man who was washing him said: Would his Grace move his arm so that I can wash his Grace? It turned out that it wasn't his arm that was in the way at all, but, by your leave, quite a different thing.'

Madame was a great blonde tomboy, Nancy Mitford says. When he first saw her, Monsieur remarked despairingly that he would never be able to manage. But by hanging holy medals in a certain place they had conceived three children. It had not been enjoyable. 'When Monsieur slept in my bed I was always obliged to lie on the very edge and often fell out in my sleep,' she grumbled. 'Monsieur couldn't bear to be touched and if I stretched out my foot and accidentally brushed against him in my sleep he would wake me up and berate me for half an hour.'

Monsieur was a swarthy fellow, with eyes like currants, one of history's sodomites, in spite of which he had two wives, one mistress and eleven legitimate children. His interests in life were clothes, jewels, parties, etiquette, *objets d'art* and boys. Once when his son, the Duc de Chartres, was asked if he liked dressing up, he said, 'I like it better than Madame does, but not as much as Monsieur.'

La Grande Mademoiselle, Anne-Marie d'Orléans, describes a ball at Monsieur's: Monsieur, Mlle de Villeroy, Mlle de Gourdon and Anne-Marie d'Orléans were dressed in silver tissue bordered with rose-coloured pipings and wore aprons of black velvet covered with red, white and black plumes, their hair was dressed to resemble the coiffure of the peasants of Bresse and they carried shepherd's crooks of red lacquer ornamented with silver. 'We thought we looked very like shepherds and shepherdesses,' Anne-Marie d'Orléans says.

Madame loved animals and lived surrounded by dogs, lame ducks, flocks of canaries and parrots. 'I don't find that parrots smell,' she wrote, 'and I

LEFT: Madame, Duchess of Orleans, 'a great blonde tomboy'. Monsieur, Duke of Orleans, who loved dressing up.

have any dogs' messes cleared away at once.' Every night she was kept warm by six little dogs all arranged around her. What she did find dirty and never could get used to were all the people stationed in the galleries in front of their rooms who relieved themselves in the corners. It was impossible to leave one's apartments, she said, without seeing somebody pissing.

Neither did she care much for clothes. Everyone at Versailles from little girls to ladies of eighty wore coiffures of ribbons, everyone that is but Madame, who said she could not bear anything on her head during the day and at night found their rustling too noisy. The coiffures were known as *Les Fontanges* after the 'stupid little' duchess who started the fashion. They started off merely as a knot of ribbon and gradually developed into huge wired constructions. Everyone was amused when a fellow called Allart left Versailles for London and news came back that he was dressing all the ladies so tall that they could not get into their sedan chairs.

When head-dresses began to be worn forward, women standing close together would get entangled and be unable to unravel themselves without help. Madame seems to have relented and adopted these, as she says she was always getting caught up with her daughter.

Madame, needless to say, had heard a great deal of talk about William of Orange's wedding when he married the Duke of York's daughter Mary. Among other things it was said that he went to bed in woollen drawers on his wedding night. When the King of England suggested that he might care to take them off he replied that since he and his wife would have to live together for a long time she would have to get used to his habits. He was accustomed to wearing his woollens and had no intention of changing now.

When Charles died, the unpopular Duke of York had come to the throne. There had followed three years of religious persecution and rebellion before James fled to France and William and Mary, woollen drawers and all, landed to take the throne. Everyone liked the poor Queen* and, though he was thought a bore, James seems to have been more popular in France (where he sat emitting heartrending sighs and planning the assassination of William) than in his own country. Everyone hated William. They considered him a usurper and the Protestant faith to be bourgeois and dreary. Louis gave James and Mary precedence over everybody, lodged them splendidly, clothed and fed them and all their scheming followers and sent James in French ships with a French army to be beaten in Ireland. James finally fell to the ground with a stroke while the choir was chanting, 'Our inheritance is turned to strangers, the crown is fallen from our head.'

*Mary of Modena. Anne Hyde had died.

LE ROY IACQUE DÉLOGE.

J'avois fait un ragoust pour tout l'Angleterre:
fans que ie me fuis trop hasté.
J'aurois demon renom rempli toutte la terre;
Mais un ORANGE a tout gâté.

A French view of 'dismal Jimmy' when James II.

Chapter 5

THE Glorious Revolution of 1688 brought major changes. The Whigs who had contrived the whole thing were taking no risks and they imposed on William and Mary the Declaration of Rights. By consenting to do nothing without approval of the cabinet the King surrendered his executive powers. The first Civil List began in 1697 although as early as 1689 parliament voted an annual sum of £60,000 to pay the salaries of ministers and judges and to cover the expenses of the royal family and their palaces.

Licentious as Charles II's court had been it was still the centre of patronage, politics, fashion, art, learning and a hundred other activities. From William and Mary onwards the court ceased as a centre of government and became inaccessible except for formal occasions of extreme dullness. Patronage was to be found elsewhere—in the lobbies of parliament and in country and London houses of political hostesses. The court was still there and everyone entitled to the entrée paid their respects regularly, but it was a matter of duty and of etiquette rather than any attraction the court possessed. Pleasure like patronage was to be found elsewhere, in small individual courts ruled by society hostesses. 'We used to sit down to dinner, a little snug party of about thirty odd, up to the chin in beef, venison, geese, turkeys, etc, and generally over the chin in claret,' Lord Hervey remembered. Whole families with their households now came to London for the Season (which lasted while parliament was sitting from February to the end of July), to be diverted by politics, plays, masquerades, dinners, gossip and, not least of all, to marry their daughters. Country cousins were exactly that, they stuck at home in the mud. The social functions of the Season were almost as important as meetings of the cabinet. A large house with a ballroom

Horace Walpole.

was essential, entertaining was on the 'cutlet for cutlet' basis, unless you gave parties you would not be invited to other people's. Then in July it would all be over, everyone packed up and returned to the country. Horace Walpole, the great gossip of the eighteenth century, did not like this at all. 'I am quite out of humour,' he wrote, 'the whole town is melted away, you never saw such a desert . . . Nothing but half a dozen private gentlewomen left, who live upon the scandal that they laid up . . .'

Queen Mary held courts and drawing rooms regularly twice a week. They were boring to both the Queen and her guests. Her invalid sister Anne was even less designed to be a leader of *haut ton*. On her death in 1714 George

Louis of Brunswick-Lüneberg became King. He was fifty-four, short, fair-skinned, with bright blue bulbous eyes. He had no time for levées and drawing rooms and preferred to spend as much time as possible in his German palace at Herrenhausen. William Hamilton, the modern anti-monarchist, especially dislikes the Hanoverians, a profligate corrupt bunch he calls them while George I is a 'dullard'. His Queen, Sophia, was interred in the castle of Ahlden until her death in 1726 (a story which provided the courts of Europe with decades of gossip) and the King brought with him a 'baggage of Valkyries' instead. Hamilton says that the King, who did not know a word of English, secured his base in the cabinet by finding 'a willing and wily tool' in Robert Walpole—England's first prime minister in the modern sense. The King turned two of the Valkyries into the Duchess of Kendal and the Countess of Dartington, and Walpole created forty dukes, packing the Commons with nominee M.P.s of the peers he had created.

In spite of being in love with his wife, by the time George II came to the throne in 1727 he had already enjoyed the favours of Mrs Howard for the best part of ten years. She was plain, deaf, modest and witty and had once sold her hair so that her husband could give an important dinner. The King liked to go to her apartments at nine o'clock most evenings and among other passions indulge in cutting out paper figures. When the Queen died of a ruptured womb, Walpole and Lord Hervey (who lived on a diet of asses' milk with a very little biscuit) advised the King to take Lady Deloraine for a mistress until another, new, Valkyrie, Madame Walmoden, could be brought from Germany. Unfortunately His Majesty said she stank so badly of Spanish wine he could not bear her. Besides being malodorous she seems to have been remarkably tactless. A great fracas reached Horace Walpole's ears when, to the amusement of the King, one of his daughters pulled Lady Deloraine's chair away as she was sitting down to cards. She, irritated by his laughter, did exactly the same to His Majesty. This was not at all a success, he was not amused and she was disgraced.

George II's courts were always of incredible dullness, alleviated only by mishaps. Everyone was delighted when poor Miss Young on making her curtsey entangled the heel of her shoe in her train and fell backwards with her legs in the air. So little kindness, so much whispering was abroad that the Marquis of Halifax observed the court was no better than a company of well-bred fashionable beggars.

London meanwhile was in the grip of diversions. Not a street was free from assemblies, spirited ladies might go to as many as seven in a night. Plays, balls and masquerades were all the fashion. 'We are all diversions', Walpole writes, 'we divert ourselves extremely.' The whole town was dressing, days

A card of invitation to Ranelagh Gardens.

were spent in preparing for subscription masquerades and then in describing them. The world would sit down to its writing desk and take up its quill. 'I must tell you how fine the masquerade of last night was,' Walpole writes. 'There were five hundred persons of the greatest variety of handsome and rich dresses I ever saw and all the jewels of London. There were to be seen Lady Conway as a charming Mary Stuart, their Graces of Richmond as Henry VIII and Jane Seymour—excessively rich and both so handsome—and all kinds of old pictures stepped from their frames.' The world it seemed was given up to rockets and masquing. Crowds of Henry the Eighths, Wolseys, Vandyke portraits and Harlequins, dozens of ugly Queens of Scots, hosts of Grecian girls, Persian sultanas and Cleopatras danced the nights away. And what dramas there were! Poor Miss Jenny, Lord Conway's sister, died suddenly from drinking lemonade at one masquerade, and Miss Chudleigh, Maid of Honour to the Princess of Wales, turned up at another as Iphigenia, so naked that the high priest could easily inspect the entrails of his victim.

The Duke and Duchess of Richmond gave wonderful fêtes: fireworks on the terrace and concerts of water music. You could not conceive a prettier sight, the gardens filled with the fashionable beau monde, the river with boats, the shores and adjacent houses with crowds and the sky with discharged rockets.

Then there was that display case of society, the opera, where it was often the audience rather than the artistes that provided the spectacle, and sometimes halted the performance altogether. 'We had a great scuffle the other night at the opera which interrupted it,' Walpole writes. 'Lord Lincoln was abused in a most shocking manner by a drunken officer, upon which he kicked him, and was drawing his sword but was prevented. I climbed into the front boxes and stepping over the shoulders of three ladies before I knew where I was, found that I had lighted in Lord Rockingham's lap.' Another evening, one of the dramatic guards fell flat on his face, motionless, in an apoplectic fit. Miss Chudleigh, who apparently had never seen a man fall flat on his face before, went into the most theatrical fit of kicking and shrieking that ever was seen. Several other ladies who were preparing their fits were so distanced that she had the whole house to herself, and such confusion for half an hour Walpole had never seen.

In May 1742 Ranelagh Gardens were opened in Chelsea. There was a vast gilt amphitheatre into which everybody that loved eating and drinking, staring or crowding was admitted for twelve pence. There were also Vauxhall Gardens. Walpole describes a frightful evening spent there by

Miss Chudleigh as Iphigenia.
OVERLEAF: A fete given by the Duke of Richmond on 15th May 1749.

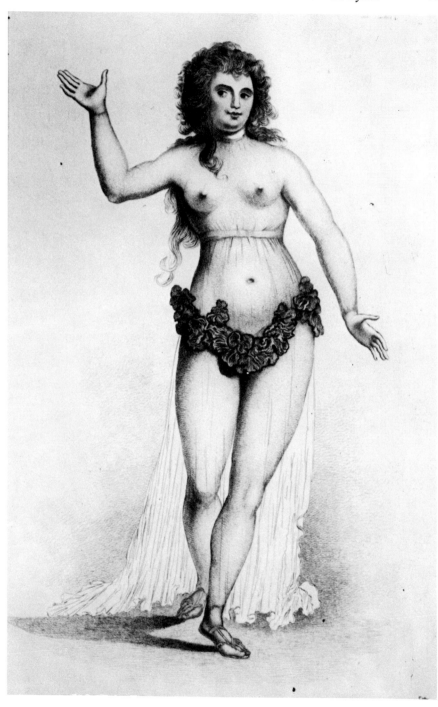

invitation of Lady Caroline Petersham. 'We issued into the Mall to assemble our company which was all the town if we could get it.' All, however, being not available they made do with the Duke of Kingston, Lord March, Mr Whitehead, a pretty Miss Beauclerc and a very foolish Miss Sparre. 'As we sailed up the Mall with all our colours flying, Lord Petersham with his hose and legs twisted to every point of crossness strode by us on the outside and repassed again on the return. "My lord, my lord! Why don't you see us?" Lady Caroline called. My lord never stirred his hat or took the least notice of anybody.' They marched to their barge, attended by a boat of French horns, and embarked at Vauxhall where a Mrs Lloyd was overheard saying loudly: 'Poor girls I am sorry to see them in such bad comapny.' On this Miss Sparre wanted a duel and took pains that Lord March should resent it: 'but he, very agreeable, laughed her out of the charming frolic.' Next they picked up Lord Granby, who had arrived drunk from an inn in Chelsea and tried to make love to poor Miss Beauclerc, who had no idea what to do with his whispers or hands. Miss Sparre, Walpole tells us, was well disposed to receive both. 'At last we assembled in our booth, Lady Caroline in the front with the vizor of her hat erect. She had fetched my brother Lord Orford from the next box to help us to mince chickens. We minced seven chickens into a china dish, which Lady Caroline stewed over a lamp with three pats of butter and a flagon of water, stirring and rattling, and laughing and we every minute expecting to have the dish fly about our ears.'

When not mincing chicken, all geniuses of the age were employed in designing new plans for desserts—a favourite being baby Vauxhall Gardens with sugar figures, illuminated by millions of little lamps. The Earl and Countess of Northumberland made the town a supper and outraged Walpole with their dessert which he thought most vulgar—a *chasse* at Herrenhausen, the rear of which was brought up by a chaise and six, containing a man with a blue riband and a lady sitting by him, presumably the King and his Valkyrie, Countess Walmoden.

A favourite topic for wagging tongues and pens was the Gunning sisters. They were Irish girls of no fortune but of such beauty (and vanity) that they made more noise than any beauty since the days of Helen. Even poor deaf Lord Chesterfield heard and talked about them. Mobs waited at doors to see them enter their sedan chairs. Once they were at Hampton Court and, as they were entering the Beauty Room (in which were hung the Kneller portraits of beauties), the housekeeper was also entering with a group. 'This way, ladies,' she was saying, 'here are the beauties.' The Gunnings flew into a rage and asked her what she meant. They had come, they said, to see the palace, not to be exhibited themselves. The younger married the Duke of Hamilton, who

The Grand Walk in Vauxhall Gardens.

was, according to Walpole, hot, debauched, extravagant, and damaged in his fortune and person. He fell in love with her at a masquerade and being impatient married her with a ring from the bed curtain. On her presentation at court everyone stood on chairs in the drawing room so that they could see her better.

The elder, Lady Coventry, was possibly the more stupid of the two, but no less beautiful. A shoemaker in Worcester made two and a half guineas by showing, at a penny a look, a shoe he was making for her. She made a great to-do when she was mobbed in Hyde Park and insisted that twelve sergeants of the guard should be available in case of riot. Off she went to the park again immediately, pretending to be frightened, and desired directly the assistance of the officer on guard, who ordered the twelve sergeants to march behind her 'and in this pomp did the idiot walk all the evening with more mob about her than ever'.

The amphitheatre at Ranelagh Gardens, 'into which everybody that loved eating and drinking, staring or crowding was admitted for twelve pence'.

The Gunning sisters, a favourite topic for wagging tongues.

London was *ce pays-là*, a village where everyone knew everyone else's business. Lord Abergavenny had killed one of his servants at Oxford; Sir John Bland had flirted away his fortune and Lord Cobham had spat into Lord Hervey's hat for a wager. Lady Hartington and Lady Rachel Walpole were brought to bed of sons, Lord Burlington and Lord Falkland had new attacks of palsies, Lady Coventry had miscarried one or two children and was going to France, and Lady Townshend and Lady Caroline Petersham had had their anniversary quarrel. Lord Coke had demolished himself very fast, was always drunk and never returned to his wife till eight in the morning. The Duke of Devonshire called his children Mrs Hopeful, Mrs Tiddle, Puss, Cat and Toe, while the Duchess had had her secular assembly and was more delightfully vulgar than anyone could imagine, complaining of the wet night and how men would dirty the rooms with their shoes and calling out to the Duke: 'Good God, my Lord! don't cut the ham, nobody will eat any . . .'

News was the spice of life. There is a story of an old Duchess of Rutland who, whenever a visitor told her some news or scandal, would call to her daughter: 'Lucy, do step into the next room and make a memorandum of what Lady Greenwich, or Lady M.M. or M.N., has been telling us.' 'Lord! Madam, to be sure it cannot be true.' 'No matter, child, it will do for news into the country.'

Any breath of marriage or romance sent everyone rushing to their writing desks. All the world seems to be eloping, Walpole would write. The freshest news in town was that the Duke of C. was running about asking all the girls possessed of money to marry him; Lord Someone had nearly married a silk stocking washer, Miss So and So's trousseau was preparing and the only other marriage on the *tapis* was Lord Morton's who was going to marry a Miss Butler, which would be a great disappointment to Lady H's family. Oh yes, and Lord Middlesex's match proved an immense fortune, 'they pretend a hundred and thirty thousand pounds . . .'

Good matches were objects of envy but bad ones were something different. Lady Henrietta Herbert furnished the tea tables with tittle-tattle by asking a priest to marry her to John Beard who sang at Drury Lane. And everyone was very shocked when Lord Rockingham's youngest sister married her footman. No one could talk of anything else for quite a while: 'it is supposed she is with child by him for they used to pass many hours together which she called teaching John the mathematics.' Then there was poor Griselda Murray whose footman tried to rape her. He was convicted and transported, but Griselda's punishment was quite as bad, her marriage prospects were ruined, a stigma was attached to her name and ballads were written about her.

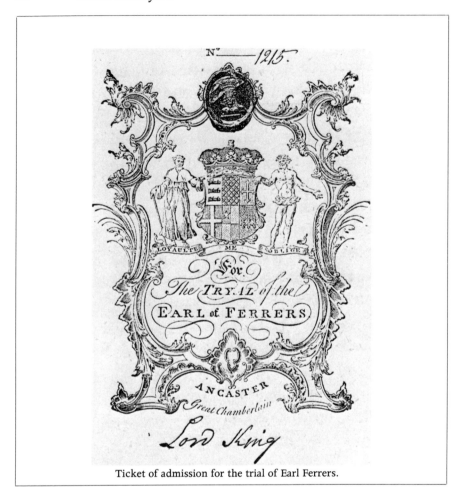

Ticket of admission for the trial of Earl Ferrers.

The whole system was geared to protecting the loss of a young girl's reputation, just as much as her virginity. Even the conversational tone differed among properly brought up people when a *jeune fille* was present. If a girl disappeared for half an hour it could mean that *something might have happened* and potential suitors would evaporate. It was the convention: all males were in search of prey and all females must be saved from deflowering. A well brought up young lady was not allowed to be alone with a man for even half an hour. Years later, Anita Leslie's grandmother won a reputation for keeping her head in a crisis when one night she accompanied her hostess and several young people to look at a picture in the library during a dance. On opening the door they perceived the shocking sight of a young lady and gentleman in full evening dress sitting together on the floor in front of the fire. Two guilty faces looked up speechless and the young people were hastily swept from the room. What *are* they doing? they wanted to know. Mending the carpet, so kind, murmured Anita Leslie's grandmother.

When Lord Ferrers was convicted of murder for shooting his steward everyone rushed along to the trial as though it were the opera. Lady Coventry was there looking as well as ever—yet they were positive she had only a few weeks to live. The Duke of York and his young brothers were in the Prince of Wales's box. The Duke of Marlborough was looking clumsy in his new robes having given his father's to his valet, and Lords Huntingdon's and Abergavenny's scarcely hung on their backs, having been used, they said, at the trial of the Queen of Scots. Never was a criminal so literally tried by his peers, Walpole remarked, for the three persons who interested themselves most in the examination—Ravensworth, Talbot and Fortescue— were all at least as mad as he. No one could talk of anything else. He had always carried pistols to bed with his wife, they said, and threatened to kill her before morning. His procession to Tyburn was a major event of the Season. Ferrers himself was dressed in his wedding clothes and driven in his own landau by his coachman, who cried all the way. He was preceded by a string of constables and a sheriff in *his* chariot, his six horses decked with ribbon. Behind came a mourning coach and six, a hearse and the Horse Guards. The scaffold was hung all with black and prepared by the family undertakers at the family's expense.

By 1759 the kingdom of beauty, Walpole reported, was in as great disorder as the kingdom of Ireland. 'My Lady Pembroke looks like a ghost—poor Lady Coventry is going to be one and the Duchess of Hamilton is so altered I do not know her. Indeed, she is big with child, and so big, that my Lady Northumberland says, it is plain she has a camel in her belly.' The following year was a fatal one for great ladies. 'Within the twelve month have gone off Lady Essex, Lady Bessborough, Lady Granby, Lady Anson and Lady Lincoln,' Walpole wrote on August 1. 'My Lady Coventry is still alive, sometimes at the point of death, sometimes recovery . . .' But by October she was dead and it was discovered that the Duchess of Hamilton had consumption too. Poor Lady Coventry had been vain to the end, lying with a pocket glass constantly in her hand and when that told her how great the change was she took to her bed and for the last fortnight had no light in her room but the lamp of the tea kettle. At last she took things in through the curtains of her bed without even suffering them to be drawn. Finally ten thousand people went to see her coffin.

The next casualty was the King, who fell dead in his water closet, and off everyone went to his funeral. The muffled drums, the tolling bells, the torchlight was all very solemn, but the charm came on entering the Abbey. The whole place was illuminated by almsmen bearing torches. People stood or sat where they could, while the yeomen struggled with the immense weight of the coffin. The Duke of Cumberland had a train five yards long, his face was bloated and distorted from a stroke, and he had an extremely bad leg on which he had to stand for nearly two hours above the mouth of the vault into which he must soon descend, yet he bore it all with a firm unaffected countenance. Not so the Duke of Newcastle who fell into a fit of crying the moment he came into the chapel and flung himself backwards into a stall, the Archbishop hovering over him with a smelling bottle. In two minutes his curiosity had overcome him and he ran about the chapel with his glass to see who was or was not there, spying with one hand and mopping his eyes with the other. The Duke of Cumberland, who was sinking with heat and his bad leg, felt himself weighed down and turning round found it was the Duke of Newcastle standing on his train to avoid the chill of the marble.

Chapter 6

GEORGE III was twenty-two when he came to the throne. His was the only court in Europe where the monarch had no mistress, and no one could imagine Queen Charlotte taking a lover.* She was a dull plain princess and they settled down to a dull plain life producing fifteen children and, in the normal run of things, two weekly drawing rooms and two yearly balls—one on the Queen's birthday. Sometimes they retired to Windsor or Richmond to lead duller lives than ever, much to the disapproval of Walpole. 'The court independent of politics makes a strange figure,' he wrote. 'The recluse life led at Richmond, which is carried to such an excess of privacy and economy that the Queen's friseur waits on them at dinner and four pounds only of beef are allowed for their soup, disgusts all sorts of people.'

The court was nothing but dowdy. Any person of doubtful character was barred and just when fashionable ladies were wearing feathered quills sixteen inches long in their hair—running round to the undertaker's to find them—the Queen excluded all plumage. No sooner were feathers no longer worn in London society than she insisted they should be assumed at court. As late as February 1818, when the poor King was raving, and no one would ordinarily have dreamt of wearing plumes or hoops, the Queen's birthday drawing room was a maze of nodding head-dresses—blue, red, violet, yellow, green and white with diamonds sparkling in them.

*According to Lady Cardigan (a hundred years later), there were rumours that Queen Charlotte and the Chevalier d'Eon had had an affair, and that George IV was the result. The Chevalier was a diplomat at the court of Louis XV and was appointed to the English Embassy as Ministre Plenipotentiare. There was so much speculation as to his sex that betting in clubs was furious and Louis recalled him, insisting on the truth, whereupon it was apparently revealed that d'Eon was a woman and henceforward was known as La Chevalière.

Queen Charlotte's dowdy birthday Ball at St. James's
Palace; just when fashionable ladies were wearing
feathered quills sixteen inches long in their hair, the
Queen excluded all plumage.

No one knew better than Fanny Burney, one of the Queen's ladies-in-waiting, how tedious the court was. 'You would never believe the many things to be studied for appearing with a proper propriety,' she wrote to her father. 'In the first place you must not cough. If you find a cough tickling your throat, you must arrest it from making any sound; if you find yourself choking with the forbearance, you must choke—but not cough. In the second place, you must not sneeze. If you have a vehement cold, you must take no notice of it, if your nose membranes feel a great irritation you must hold your breath. If a sneeze still insists upon making its way, you must oppose it by keeping your teeth grinding together, if the violence of the repulse breaks some blood-vessel, you must break the blood-vessel but not sneeze. In the third place you must not on any account stir either hand or foot. If by chance a black pin runs into your head you must not take it out. If the pain is very great you must be sure to bear it without wincing, if it brings the tears to your eyes you may not wipe them off. If they give you a tingling by running down your cheeks you must look as it nothing was the matter. If the blood should gush from your head by means of the black pin, you must let it gush . . . If however the agony is very great, you may probably bite the inside of your cheek, or of your lips for a little relief . . . If you even gnaw a piece out it will not be minded only to be sure either to swallow it, or commit it to a corner of the inside of your mouth.'

The draught occupied much of courtiers' conversation. 'Let's see,' General Goldsworthy would calculate, 'how many blasts must you have every time you go to the Queen? First one upon opening your door; then another, as you get down the three steps from it, then a third as you turn the corner to enter the passage, then you come plump upon another from the hall door, then comes another fit to knock you down as you turn to the upper passage, then just as you turn towards the Queen's room comes another. At last a whiff from the King's stairs enough to blow you half a mile off. All that running along those cold passages, bursting into rooms fit to bake you, then out again into all those agreeable puffs. Bless us! there must be wind enough to carry a man of war.' And the colds—'off they drop one by one—first the Queen deserts us, then the Princess Royal begins coughing; then Princess Augusta gets the snuffles; and all the poor attendants drop off like so many snuffs of candles, dwindle, dwindle, dwindle' till at last there was not a soul in chapel but the King, the parson and General Goldsworthy, all freezing it out together.

When colds and draughts failed there was always awful Mrs Schwellenburg and her frogs.

Fanny Burney.

Major Price: 'You must know, Colonel Gwynn, Mrs Schewellenburg keeps a pair of frogs.'

'Of frogs? Pray what do they feed upon?'

'Flies, sir,' she answered.

'And pray, ma'am, what food have they in winter?'

'Nothing other. But I can make them croak when I will,' she added, 'when I only go so to my snuff-box, knock, knock, knock, they croak all what I please.'

'Very pretty indeed,' exclaimed Colonel Goldsworthy.

'I thought to have some spawn,' she continued, 'but Lady Maria Caillon, what you call Lady Doncaster, came and frightened them. I was never so angry.'

Fanny Burney describes an outing to Oxford which illustrates the tedium and fatigue of it all. On arrival at Christ Church a cold collation was preparing for their Majesties and the Princesses. The Duchess of Ancaster and Lady Harcourt stood behind the chairs of the Queen and Princess Royal. There were no other ladies of sufficient rank to officiate for Princesses Augusta and Elizabeth. Lord Harcourt stood behind the King's chair and the Vice Chancellor and Master of Christ Church with salvers in their hands stood near the table ready to hand the 'noble waiters' whatever was wanted. Meanwhile everyone else stood at the other end of the room making a semi-circle, all facing the royal collationers. Tea, coffee and chocolate were conveyed to a large table behind the semi-circle, and all the group backed near so that one at a time might feed, screened by the semi-circle. Eating in front of the royal circle was as much *hors d'usage* as sitting down, coughing or sneezing. In turn they withdrew and some ladies even sat down to rest their twisted ankles and fatigued backs. Lady Charlotte Bertie was most valiant, in spite of her sprained ankle she began a march backwards, perfectly upright, without a stumble, right down the middle of a long apartment—poor Fanny Burney was not so expert and had to glide to the wainscot and pace a few steps backwards at a time, disentangling her train from the heels of her shoes. At another college they managed to slip into a small parlour to rest for a moment and one gentleman produced from 'a paper repository' apricots and bread. Suddenly the door opened and in came the Queen. Up they all had to start, cramming their pockets with bread and squeezing the fruit into their hands.

The King's brother, Henry Duke of Cumberland, more than made up for the monarch's dullness. Among the aristocracy there was a code. Once you had married and provided your husband with an heir it did not matter what you did so long as you did it with discretion and *were not found out.* 'Never comment on a likeness,' was an axiom of polite behaviour. Everyone knew that the Duke of Devonshire had two children by Lady Elizabeth Foster and that they all lived at Devonshire House *en famille* with Mrs Tiddle, Puss, Toe and company. But the affair was conducted with propriety and there was no scandal. The Duke of Cumberland, however, not only broke the code but his affairs caused the passing of the Royal Marriage Act and were *reported in the newspapers,* something that was practically unheard of in those days. In 1770 he was before the King's Bench accused of having 'criminal conversation' (adultery) with Lady Grosvenor. Lord Grosvenor was exceptionally rich, his money coming from the development of fashionable Mayfair, nevertheless he sued the Duke, who was in the navy at the time, for £100,000. Letters were published, without punctuation, in the papers. 'I then prayed for you my dearest love kissed your dearest little hair and lay down and dreamt of you had you on the dear little couch ten thousand times:' lines which inspired the following composition:

God bless my dearest little dear
The wind is not quite fair
From Portland Road I write this here
God bless your little hair
Doodle doodle doodle do (and so on)

Lord Grosvenor, everyone learnt, was not only rich but dull. He would sit for half an hour with his eyes fixed on a table or a chair, then apply to anybody near at hand: did they know which mare such a filly was out of? For Lady Grosvenor life in the country was tedious, the eating, riding and playing at 'stupified cards' was only alleviated by receiving 'dearest passages' written by her 'dearest soul' in lemon or milk. It was better in London. Mary Reda, an obliging widow, kept a milliner's shop in Pall Mall and hired out upstairs rooms to the best people. Another widow, Countess Dunhoff, let them meet in Cavendish Square, but would wander in unexpectedly and surprise them making love. Everyone learnt that they had often stayed together in inns when travelling between London and Cheshire. The Duke would dress as a farmer and wear a black wig. Sometimes he would appear as a young squire disordered in his senses and would be known at the various hostelries as the fool. It all ended in the White Hart, St Albans, when one of Lord Grosvenor's butlers broke down the door to find her ladyship with her breasts bare and the Duke trying to button up his waistcoat.

More noise was provided in 1769 by Miss Chudleigh. 'This far inspired innocence who is but fifty' married the Duke of Kingston, with satin

Caricature of the Duke of Cumberland and Lady Grosvenor being surprised by Countess Dunhoff.

Representation of the Trial of the Dutchess of Kingston.

wedding dress, Brussels lace, pearls and all. According to Walpole, the Duke
had kept her openly for almost twenty-five years and by marrying her would
recover half his fortune which he had lavished on her. Unfortunately it
seemed that she was already married, with a son. ('Do you know?' she once
said to Lord Chesterfield. 'The world says I have twins.' 'Does it?' he replied.
'I make a point of believing only one-half of what the world says.') Seven
years later all tongues were busy with her Grace who was being had up for
bigamy. Tickets for her trial were much in demand. 'Mrs Garrick and I were
in full dress by seven,' Mrs Hannah More wrote. 'You will imagine the bustle
of five thousand people getting into one hall.'

During the eighteenth century the national press began its invasion of
private lives. Pepys and his friends had known the gossip, but by word of
mouth, nothing was published unless you could count Rochester's
lampoons. Now defamations could be ventilated through ballads, broad-
sheets and newspapers for the public to stare at, although it was mostly the
goings-on of the *demi-monde* that made the news. The *Town and Country
Magazine* writes for example of Mrs Armistead, the daughter of a man who
earned 'a very decent livelihood in the shoe trade', a tall genteel lady with a
beautiful face and captivating eyes—a notable bawd. The Duke of Grafton,
Charles II's grandson, was often seen with her, also a leading Whig peer, the
young Earl of Derby, who had thrown out his wife because of her amours
with—the Duke of Grafton, who was known as Black Harry and had
inherited many of his grandfather's lustier characteristics. He lived with
Nancy Parsons, a notorious lady, who called herself Mrs Hoghton—'the
Duke of Grafton's Mrs Hoghton, the Duke of Dorset's Mrs Hoghton,
everybody's Mrs Hoghton,' declared Walpole. Grafton maintained no
decorum. Everyone was appalled when he took Mrs Hoghton to the opera
while his wife was there and paid no attention to anyone but Nancy. Mrs
Cornelly's in Soho Square smacked also of the *demi-monde*. Rumour had it
that forty beds were made and unmade every day. The masquerades after
supper were the talk of the town and marked by hard drinking and lewd
singing. The windows would be flung open and the mob pelted with half-
empty bottles and the remains of supper. The *London Magazine* and the
Gentlemen's Intelligencer ranted against the bad behaviour, luxury and
extravagance.

Public disapproval made no impression on the Season. The vast rooms of
Grosvenor and Berkeley Squares with their marble columns and gilded
capitals continued to blaze night after night with candles and resound with

Miss Chudleigh on trial as Duchess of Kingston.

A satire against extravagant hairstyles and the deadly practice of painting faces.

flutes, fiddles and oboes as successions of people passed up the great stairways to divert themselves. Lord Eglington dispensed nearly £80,000 in an attempt to revive a pageant from the Middle Ages and Comte d'Adhéman gave a brilliant ball to which fourteen of the most distinguished beauties came as 'Les Filles de Minerve' in uniforms of celestial blue satin covered with spangles and laced down the seams with superb embroidery.

To be fashionable was to be doing things ever later in the day than the rest of the world. Ladies must be huge; ballooning vast and voluminous below the waist, their dresses, petticoats and panniers spreading over wide compressible rings of whalebone; towering with enormous accumulations of horsehair on the head (for which wire contraptions were sold to keep out the mice) stiffened with pomatum, filled with powder and adorned with bunches of vegetables, sometimes so large that ladies were compelled to ride with their heads out of carriage windows or kneeling down. Faces were blanched with white lead, which, together with the red paint used on cheeks, was believed to have caused the death of many fine ladies—Lady Coventry being one. There is a story of her husband chasing her round and round the dinner table so that he could catch her and scrub her face with a table napkin.

Like their uncle the King's sons had grown up to be most unsatisfactory. The Duke of York was so extravagant that he had caused a public clamour,

Frederick, Duke of York, with his mistress Mary Clarke.

'Prinny.'

and he connived at the activities of his mistress, Mary Clarke, a *demi-mondaine* who dealt in commissions like a broker; the public exposure was carried out in the glare of a House of Commons inquiry, his army career came to a halt and he spent the rest of his life pursuing the elderly Duchess of Rutland and building palaces he could not afford. The Duke of Clarence was a sailor who lived on dry land in debt with ten children and Mrs Jordan whom he finally sacked to marry Princess Adelaide. The Duke of Kent was a martinet whose love of punishments made him the most hated man in the army and who lived with his French mistress Madame St Laurent; after twenty-two years he also sacked her to marry a princess and father Queen Victoria. The Duke of Cambridge was untypical in that he lived within his income and only begat legitimate children; he was given to answering any rhetorical questions included in the sermon in a loud bellowing voice. Ernest, Duke of Cumberland was the most unsavoury of all; by the time he died the public believed that he had fathered a child by his sister, Princess Sophia, and murdered his valet.

As for the Prince of Wales—Prinny—the King viewed his development with much distaste. Life at home had been dull. To divert himself he drank hard, swore publicly round the palace drawing room and as soon as the King had gone to bed he and the Duke of York went out debauching in brothels or spent the night with their mistresses. The Prince had been steered into Perdita Robinson's skilled hands. She was an actress, who had been set up in Clarges Street by Lord Malden, and who drove about in a silk-lined carriage

Georgiana, Duchess of Devonshire.

with an entwined cypher on the side resembling a coat of arms. Her box at the opera was fitted up, like the Queen of France's, as an elegant salon and was surrounded by distinguished beaux. What with one thing and another the Prince was often ill and there were plenty of insinuating caricatures in the newspapers. When he took to keeping a French dancer a certain disorder broke out. Cartoons of the Prince showed bottles of venereal nostrums at his bedside.

His great friend was Charles James Fox. Both were large florid men with a tendency to fat and recklessness with money. With Fox as his unofficial prime minister, the Prince became monarch of the Whigs. His parties at Carlton House were astonishing. 'My dearest mother,' wrote the young Irish poet Thomas Moore, 'I ought to have written yesterday, but I was in bed all day after the fête, which I did not leave till past six in the morning. Nothing was ever half so magnificent.'

The Duchess of Devonshire was one of Fox's most ardent canvassers and a famous Whig hostess. Soon there were rumours associating her with the Prince of Wales. A cartoon inspired by ballooning shows the Duchess and the Prince standing face to face in the balloon basket.

Prince: 'It rises majestically.'
Duchess: 'Yes I feel it.'

Gossip had it that the baby the Duchess gave birth to in 1785 was the Prince's.

The Gothic conservatory at Carlton House.

Carlton House, according to Walpole, was perfect, but where the money was to come from to pay for it he could not conceive, all the tin mines in Cornwall would not pay a quarter. The tin mines would certainly have come in to pay off the Prince's debts which were by now colossal. He had lost several thousand pounds betting on twenty turkeys racing against twenty geese, and another expense was Perdita Robinson, who was trying to blackmail him. The King refused to help, the Prince married Mrs Fitzherbert, closed Carlton House and drove off in a cab to Brighton where he continued to entertain his friends lavishly. Everyone wrote from the Pavilion complaining ungratefully that the heat made them languid, their gout was

Ballroom at Brighton Pavilion.

appalling and all the syllabubs, meringues and ices made them bilious. In 1795 the Prince gave up Mrs Fitzherbert and, to get his debts paid off, married Caroline of Brunswick who was flamboyant and dirty and appalled her fastidious husband. He managed to consummate the marriage (with it was said the help of cantharides) then departed, having as little to do with

Lady going to a ball in 1796.

her as he possibly could. Unfortunately his unhappy domestic life made the Prince more unpopular than ever.

With all this strain the King had deteriorated. After one levée he had snatched off Sir George Baker's wig and shown his backside to the retinue. A pamphlet, *History of the Royal Malady*, tells of a drive in Windsor Park. Suddenly the King shouted, 'There he is,' handed the reins to the Queen and hurried over to an oak tree. Bowing respectfully he seized one of the lower branches and shook it. The Queen turned pale, there apparently was the King of Prussia. When the royal carriage was once more underway, with the Queen, the Princess Royal and two maids of honour sitting in embarrassed silence, the King, according to the pamphlet, said: 'Charlotte, will you give me leave to XXXX XXX.'

On good days he would sing songs, play hornpipes and dance with his doctors. On bad days he was fastened into a straitjacket. Occasionally he would recover enough to attend the palace drawing rooms. By now the whole of London society was split into Tory and Whig camps, and hostesses took care not to mix the two. Whig ladies wore hats with the Prince's symbols, a triple ostrich feather and the words 'Ich Dien'; and Tories wore bandeaus saying 'God save the King'. At the first palace drawing room after the King's recovery the Queen refused to look at such Whigs as Fox, Burke and Sheridan and glared at the Duchess of Devonshire and Lady Duncannon, who were almost the only ladies in the room not sporting bandeaus. The rush to display loyalty caused such a tumult that 'one heard nothing but screams and women carrying out in fits', according to the bandeauless Lady Duncannon. 'The whole ground was strewed with pearls and diamonds crumbled to pieces.'

Soon after her marriage the Princess of Wales began to behave scandalously. She could not bear what she called good society. Her parties were not popular, her dinners were long and as for her music it was procured only for the sake of making a noise—cats would have done as well. At the opera she talked so loudly that it was impossible to hear the performance. Her morals caused such concern that the 'Delicate Investigation' was set up, its chief object being to determine the paternity of a child called William Austin, who grew up under the Princess's protection, slept in her bedroom till he was fourteen, lived in her house until she died and was then incarcerated in a lunatic asylum. It was a relief when in 1814 the Princess left the country and went off to live with an Italian adventurer called Pergami, who had been a general's valet. Everyone in Genoa was suddenly surprised to see a gilt and mother of pearl phaeton resembling a sea shell being drawn through the streets by two piebald horses driven by a child in flesh-coloured tights. The Princess sat in the phaeton, fat and forty, wearing a pink hat, pink feathers floating in the wind, a low pink bodice and a short white skirt showing two fat legs and a pair of top boots. Preceding the phaeton was Pergami dressed as King Murat.

When, in 1820, poor George III died at last, to everyone's horror, Caroline returned, red-faced, hard-drinking, wearing a black wig and all set for the coronation. She was received by ecstatic crowds cheering themselves into a

Cartoon of Queen Caroline and
Pergami in Italy.
OPPOSITE:
'Nothing like it has been seen
since the Tudors': Caroline
returning from the House of
Lords, cheered by the mob.

riot. The government took proceedings and the new Queen was accused of
adultery and scandalous behaviour. Nothing like it had been seen since the
Tudors. Each day the Queen drove, cheered by the mob, to the House of
Lords. Each day London and the provinces read in the newspapers a long and
sordid account of her goings-on. Meanwhile George IV, an immense bulk of a
man, squeezed into shape by corsets, and detested by most of his subjects,
lurked at Windsor with his latest mistress Lady Conyngham. To seduce his
people he planned a most splendid coronation which carried no provision for
the Queen. She appeared on the day, regardless, dressed in white and
escorted by Lord Hood, an ex-lover, to be turned away at the door. The King,
it was thought, behaved very badly at his coronation banquet, nodding and
winking at Lady Conyngham. Two weeks later Caroline died. George IV
spent his last nine years with Lady Conyngham: 'Not an idea in her head,
nothing but a hand to accept pearls and diamonds with, and an enormous
balcony to wear them on,' the Russian ambassador's wife said.

Certainly she was mercenary and was called by one paper 'Cunning Ham'.
On the death of George IV one of the pages revealed that she had constantly
asked the King for the key which he wore round his neck, and which she
supposed opened a closet containing valuables. The page had left the room

for a moment, he said, and returned to find Lady Conyngham struggling to get the key off the body. Lady Brownlow records that the Conyngham carriage left loaded with packages of all shapes and sizes. She took clocks and china and was supposed to have extracted several jewels from the crown. A caricature shows her pushing a wheelbarrow away laden with pots and kettles.

Chapter 7

LONDON society was greatly influenced by the French court all through the eighteenth century. People crossed the Channel, visited Versailles and brought back the latest fashions, recipes and *bons mots*. Lady Hervey proudly carried back a tin funnel covered with green ribbon to wear for keeping her bouquet fresh. 'I fear Lady Caroline and some others will catch frequent colds and sore throats with overturning the reservoir,' Walpole had written. Lady Caroline Petersham and Lady Coventry had gone off together to Paris expecting to take the city by storm but had been disappointingly received. The French could not conceive that Lady Caroline had ever been handsome nor that Lady Coventry had any pretence to be so. But the French craze continued. Meat was disguised by French cooks, and people affected a strange tongue of broken English, mangled French and fashionable rolling R's. *Valets de chambre* were brought over to curl hair, mount desserts and occasionally to announce visits. French maids were appointed. Letters were published in newspapers from gentlemen complaining that they had been inveigled at enormous expense into taking their wives and daughters to Paris and that they returned covered with ridiculous frippery, their hair dyed blue and packed with a complication of shredded velvet, feathers, ribands and false stones of a thousand colours.

As for France itself, news filtered through of the distress of the nation and the greatness of the court's diversions. 'Madame de Pompadour is continually busied in finding new journeys and diversions to keep him [Louis XV] from falling into the hands of the clergy,' Walpole wrote. 'The last party she made for him was a stag-hunting; the stag was a man dressed in skin and horns, worried by 12 men dressed like blood hounds.' Walpole needless to say visited France several times (his great heroine was Madame de

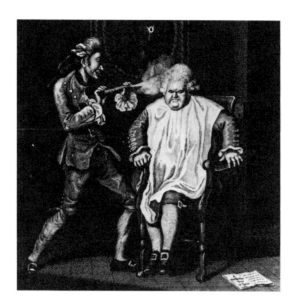

The Englishman in Paris.

Sévigné) but wrote to complain that he was famished for want of clean victuals, comfortable tea and bread and butter. En route to Paris in the sixties he found Boulogne so plump, the country around so wonderfully enriched, that he put it down to the English swarming their way to the capital. He himself encountered a coach and four with a lady in pea-green, a smart hat and feather and two *suivantes*: 'My reason told me it was the Archbishop's concubine, but luckily my heart whispered that it was Lady Mary Coke'— separated from her nasty husband. What struck Walpole was the total difference in manners between the French and the English—although it seems to have been mainly the idiosyncracies of hats that caught his attention. 'Servants carry their lady's train and put her into the coach with their hat on. They walk about the streets in the rain with umbrellas to avoid putting on their hats, driving themselves in open chaises in the country without hats in the rain too and yet often wear them in a chariot in Paris when it does not rain. The very footmen are powdered from the breath of day and yet wait behind their master as I saw the Duc of Praslin's do with a red pocket handkerchief about their necks. Versailles, like everything else, is a mixture of parade and poverty, and in every instance exhibits something most dissonant from our manners. In the colonnades, upon the staircases, nay in the antechambers of the royal family, there are people selling all sorts of wares. While we were waiting in the Dauphin's sumptuous bedchamber, till his dressing room door should be opened, two fellows were sweeping it, and dancing about in sabots to rub the floor.'

Walpole was presented the year after Madame de Pompadour's death. The Queen took great notice of him, none of the rest said a syllable. 'You are let into the King's bedchamber just as he has put on his shirt; he dresses and talks good-humouredly to a few, glares at strangers, goes to mass, to dinner, and a-hunting.' The 'good old Queen' was at her dressing table attended by two or three old ladies. Thence you went to the Dauphin. 'He scarce stays a minute, indeed, poor creature, he is a ghost, and cannot possibly last three months.' The Dauphine was in her bedchamber, looked cross, and was not civil. The four Mesdames were clumsy, plump old wenches and stood in a bedchamber in a row with black cloaks and knotting bags wriggling as if they wanted to make water. That ceremony too was very short. Then you were carried to the Dauphin's three boys 'who you may be sure only bow and stare'. The Duc de Berry [later Louis XVI] looked weak and weak-eyed. The Comte de Provence was a fine boy, the Comte d'Artois well enough. The whole concluded with seeing the Dauphin's little girl dine, who was as round and as fat as a pudding.

He was there again in 1771, writing back, 'The distress here is incredible, especially at court. The King's tradesmen are ruined, his servants starving, even angels and archangels cannot get their pensions and salaries, but sing woe! woe! woe! instead of Hosannahs.'

In spite of this the court continued and Louis XVI came to the throne. But the reign of Louis XV had corrupted the nobility, Madame de la Tour du Pin writes in her memoirs, and every form of vice could be found among the court nobles. Virtue was considered provincial. Madame de la Tour du Pin's marriage and presentation were among the last. Her trousseau cost 45,000 francs. She was married on a Monday and presented the following Sunday. It was impossible, she says, to conceive of anything so ridiculous as that rehearsal. The dancing master, his hair well-dressed and white with powder, wore a billowing underskirt and stood at one end of the room representing the Queen. Madame, who wore a train and the wide panniers of court dress above and below her morning dress, must raise her glove and kiss the hem of the Queen's gown.

Presentation always took place after mass on Sunday *'en grands corps'*. She wore a splendid bodice without shoulders, laced at the back, showing a

Madame de Pompadour.

chemise of fine lawn through which it could easily be seen if the skin were not white. From the top of the arm to the elbow fell three or four flounces of blond lace, the throat was bare though partly covered by seven or eight rows of diamonds lent by the Queen. The front of the bodice was as though laced with diamonds, and on the back more diamonds again. The dress was all in white, the entire skirt embroidered with pearls and silver. She made three curtseys, removed her glove, received the accolade and found the whole performance exceedingly embarrassing, disliking to receive such prolonged and intense stares from the whole court.

These Sunday courts were always the same. A few minutes after midday the ladies would enter the salon. The audience lasted until twenty minutes to one and then the procession moved off to Mass, the ladies following in order of rank, four or five abreast. The young ones and those who were considered in fashion on the outside taking care to walk close enough to the lines of courtiers to hear the things that were being whispered to them. One needed great skill to walk through that room without treading on the train of the lady in front, the feet never raised from the ground, sliding over the parquet in those little steps. Then there was dinner, a small rectangular table laid with two places, two large armchairs placed side by side, the backs high enough to screen completely the persons seated in them. Then in front a semi-circle of stools placed for the duchesses, princesses and other ladies whose office entitled them to this privilege. Behind them stood all the other ladies facing the King and Queen. The King would eat heartily, the Queen neither removed her gloves nor her napkin. As soon as the King had drunk his wine everyone curtseyed and left. Then came the race to pay court to the royal princes and princesses, who dined later. Each visit lasted three or four minutes. Then everybody stayed quietly in their rooms so as not to disarrange their hair before dining at three o'clock. After dinner, there would be conversation. It was the fashion to complain, to be weary and tired of everything.

Soon there was plenty to complain about. 'The uproar is begun in Paris,' wrote Walpole in April 1791, 'everybody that can is leaving.' People all over Europe watched horrified, taking up their quills and scratching the dreadful news, peppering it with exclamation marks, that the King, the Queen and most of the nobility, those who could not escape, had lost everything: their land and their lives.

Leaving the French Opera.
OVERLEAF: A Parisian soirée.

Queen Marie-Antoinette.

Chapter 8

T HE French and American Revolutions set in motion new forces and democratic ideas. The English nobility during the nineteenth century had been a politically effective class, the system working by patronage and influence. The peerage remained a small body—161 temporal peers in 1704, 182 in 1780. The largest single group consisted of men ennobled for service to the state, like Walpole and Pitt, lawyers like Cowper and Harcourt and soldiers like Cobham and Cadogan. Up until the Reform Bill in 1837 candidates for government appointments or seats in Parliament had to possess a certain amount of land. It was property that the old parliament represented. The reformers wanted people to be the subject of repre-sentation. One man: one vote. Men like Cobbett deplored the rise of a new more irresponsible profit-making class of landed gentry, which drew its wealth from trade and finance. It was the difference between an aristocracy attached to the soil and a new people with no relish for country matters, who looked to the soil only for its rents and viewed it as an object of speculation. The first thing the *nouveaux riches* did was to buy land, thus purchas-ing the aristocratic pursuits of hunting, shooting and fishing. Land was the aerodrome from which to rise in the social scale. In the middle of the century railways brought a new mobility and the railway promoters themselves became socially significant. (Queen Victoria herself was entertained by Hudson the railway king; Mrs Hudson would say to her maid: 'Dress me for ten, dress me for twenty.') From the moment the Lords passed the Reform Bill, Disraeli said, the aristocratic principle of government expired forever.

Under George III the House of Lords had become a Tory stronghold. The nineteenth-century House of Lords started almost fifty percent larger in size than the normal eighteenth-century one had been. Peerages became the

Lady Dorothy Nevill: during her lifetime she saw a change in the whole standard of living—in her view for the worse.

accepted method of royal reward for services rendered, and the regular way of ensuring governmental influence. The Tory party became identified with opposition to radical movements and political reform and clung to hierarchical and aristocratic notions of society.

The Season continued in an established routine through the nineteenth century until the Great War. Like the spring it returned each year. The winter session would assemble in February bringing to London the legislators and their wives. Entire households would travel to London from all corners of Britain. The carriages, the coachmen, grooms, footmen, butlers, head housekeepers and their minions would come up from the country. Then neither late nor early, on the 1st of May, as regular as clockwork, it burst into full bloom. The houses of Mayfair and Belgravia would be freshly painted, the window-boxes filled with flowers, and while the children lived at the top of the house doing the same old lessons with the same old governesses, fräuleins and mademoiselles, their parents, elder brothers and sisters cavorted—although sometimes the drains were not too good and everyone would go down with sore throats and diphtheria. Writing letters, riding and driving in the park occupied the mornings, while the leaving of cards—not to speak of *visites de digestion* which every young man was supposed to pay—took up most afternoons. Thus society remained more or less unchanged until the 1890s. It was more like a large family than anything else, Lady Dorothy Nevill remembers, and a brilliant family it was too—an assemblage of people who either by birth, intellect or aptitude were ladies and gentlemen in the true sense of the word. Money-making was left to another class.

Memoirs of the nineteenth century are filled with balls, theatres and parties. Lady Dorothy Nevill remembers going to fifty balls, sixty parties, thirty dinners and twenty-five breakfasts. To be brought out meant having one's hair up, accompanying one's parents to dinner parties and balls and being presented to the Queen. There were no entertainments given especially, young people were merely allowed to attend the ordinary parties given for royalty, statesmen and politicians (the word debutante was coined only in 1837). The nearest thing to special balls had been the subscription affairs at Almacks, admission to which all through the eighteenth century being as much of an object as a seat in the Privy Council—to be admitted to Almacks meant that your *ton* was stamped and you were one of the exclusive set. Tiers of seats were built at one end to contain all the dowagers and chaperones and there had once been a terrible to-do when they had collapsed.

Overnight one was magically transformed from a child to a grown-up person. One stepped straight from the schoolroom to the ballroom. Princess Marie Louise describes coming down to dinner at Balmoral and finding herself sitting next to the Lord Chancellor. It was the duty of young princesses—indeed of all well brought up young ladies—to entertain their neighbours at table. Girls were not expected to know but to amuse. It was not amusing to mention servants, children, illness or money—these were all subjects which ruined conversation. True to tradition, girls must never be alone. By day they were accompanied by their maid, by night by their chaperone. Young unmarried ladies attending balls and dancing parties should never leave their chaperones between dances. If a man wished to secure a partner he was obliged to go to the chaperone and immediately lead her straight back at the end of a dance.

It was quite possible to married during one's first season—out of the schoolroom and into the castle by October. Trousseaus, Lady Dorothy Nevill remembers, were provisions for a lifetime. People laid in enormous stocks when they married. When the Duchess of Somerset died there was a wonderful sale of her trousseau. The catalogue alone was a work of art. One large room was full of silk stockings in bundles of a dozen tied with pink ribbon which had never been undone since they had been bought. Another

Banquet at Buckingham Palace—
there was no possibility of
conversation across the table if
one's neighbours were dull.

room was full of silk petticoats and dozens of dresses. There was a splendid court train and an immense collection of bonnets—some of them poke, others with plumes of feathers starting from the crown.

After one's marriage it was supposed to be quite extraordinary, if not actually embarrassing, to mix with one's friends for at least a month. Shortly after her marriage to Lord Randolph Churchill in the 1870s Jennie Jerome was presented to Czar Alexander II at a ball at Stafford House. On being told she had married only a few weeks before, he exclaimed, with a look of censure, '*Et ici déjà.*'

Jennie Jerome remembers that the London Season was looked upon as a serious matter which no self-respecting person in society would forego. Dinners, balls and parties succeeded one after another without intermission until the end of July. Parties were arranged for Hurlingham to see the pigeon shooting, for fashionable flower shows and for Wimbledon to see the shooting for the Election shield—a major feature of the Season. Then there was Rotten Row. Between midday and two o'clock the park was the most frequented place in London, the fashionable world congregated there to ride, drive or walk. Mounted on beautiful horses, the ladies wore close-fitting braided habits, the men frock coats, pearl-grey trousers and varnished boots. Many were the delightful balls, Jennie Jerome remembers, which lasted until five in the morning. Masked balls were much in vogue. Sundays, she said, were very dull. The fashion of going to the country at weekends was not known and it was not until the '80s that people began to give dinner parties on Sundays.

Queen Victoria's court was never amusing. The sparkle was to be found surrounding Prince Edward and the Marlborough House Set and in the houses of the political hostesses. The Duchess of Manchester and the Duke of Sutherland were foundation members of the 'fast set', whose gambling soirées at Manchester House horrified Queen Victoria. Right up until the Great War political hostesses were a dominant factor in English politics. Trained almost from birth in the art of entertaining, they provided, both in town and country, a rendezvous where men of all opinions could meet to discuss the affairs of the day. They exercised power largely through their influence with other ladies. A man might start his political career with every intention of being independent but if he proved too difficult there were many ways of bringing him to heel, most effective being to cut him off from the social centre. This did not necessarily matter to him but it did to his wife and daughters.

To be seen at a reception given by the Duchesses of Buccleuch or Devonshire, the Countess of Derby, or the Ladies Lansdowne or Palmerston

Louisa, Duchess of Manchester, then of Devonshire—the discreet Double Duchess.

was enough to establish the social position of any man or woman. In its time, Lady Palmerston's was the salon, *par excellence*, in Europe, there you heard all the *bons mots*, anecdote and gossip, while at the beginning of the century there had been Lady Jersey, who was called Silence by her friends, and whose house in Berkeley Square was the centre of the Tory party. Against her was Lady Holland, a redoubtable Whig hostess, who was *divorced*. Lady Harriet Granville had a wonderful description of her family spotting the newly married Lady Holland at the opera. 'My aunt moved all her fingers at once—Mr and Mrs Peterson who were there made signs. Lady Liz [the Duke of Devonshire's mistress] twisted her shawl with a forbidding glance. Caroline held up her head a little higher than usual, John reddened and I who did not know who she was thought it was strange that a poor lady looking so demure and quiet, should cause such evident confusion.' That had been in the 1790s and soon she was no longer demure but terrorising everybody, 'the only really undisputed monarchy in Europe,' wrote Lady Harriet, who had seen her again sitting in a corner at Lady Cowper's: 'throne and footstool, courtiers, and *dames d'honneur* all *dans les règles*.' She invited herself to stay at Brocket with Lord Melbourne and upset the household by installing herself exactly as if she were at home. Her windows were surrounded by magnolia, every blossom of which Lady Holland ordered to be cut within twenty-four hours.

One of the great hostesses was Queen Victoria's Mistress of the Robes, Duchess Harriet, wife of the 2nd Duke of Sutherland. She gave grand and brilliant receptions in Stafford House. In 1859 a party of Spitalfield silk weavers, whose business was badly depressed, called at Stafford House to ask if the Duchess would show her friends a new coloured silk they had christened 'Magenta'. The Duchess ordered the stuff to be made into a dress which she wore to all important functions. The new Magenta at once became fashionable. The Queen followed the example of her Mistress of the Robes, society followed the Queen and within a few weeks the looms of Spitalfield were working night and day.

The social whirl must often have been boring. Disraeli is supposed to have entertained 450 different people to dinner in one week, while Sir William Harcourt once dined out a whole week in advance of his invitations, not discovering his error until the Friday night when his hostess told him he had been expected the following Friday. Lady Stanley who spent most afternoons receiving visitors was overheard by her grandson muttering: 'Fools are so fatiguin'.'

Sometimes after leaving the dinner table ladies would not see the gentlemen again that evening. Lord John Russell was notorious for this. Fresh bottles of port (together with the chamber-pots) would be brought out, doors locked and every man would drink until most were under the table. It was a regular custom for the valets to come in around midnight and carry out their masters. Sometimes everyone was put in the wrong carriages and escorted to the wrong houses.

Society had strict rules and conventions to which one either conformed or one was cast out and not invited to a good party again. Louisa, Duchess of Manchester, who was an important, respected and feared hostess, and Lord Hartington were long-standing lovers of the greatest propriety. She always called him Lord So and So, while he addressed her as Duchess. They were so discreet that they were invited to dinner parties together and treated like an engaged couple—indeed when the Duke of Manchester died they married. Lady Londonderry, also one of the important political hostesses of her day, was not so lucky. As Lady Theresa Chetwynd Talbot, daughter of the 19th Earl of Shrewsbury, she had been suitable material for the Marquis of Londonderry. Within four years she had produced two sons and one daughter, within ten she had fallen in love with Henry Cust. All might have been well if Lady de Grey had not been in love with Henry Cust as well and in a fit of jealousy had wrapped up Lady Londonderry's love letters and sent

Harriet, Duchess of Sutherland, one of the great hostesses.

them round by special footman to Lord Londonderry. He had known nothing about the affair and his pride would not take the shock. There was no divorce, no scandal, but the marriage was over: 'henceforth we do not speak,' he said to his wife. From then on he never addressed a word to her again, except for necessary announcements in public. They arrived separately at balls and operas and received in silence at their political receptions.

Lady Cardigan tells the story of a friend who was crossing one of London's smart squares and noticed that straw was being laid down on all four sides—the custom being that if some important person were ill, straw was laid outside the house to deaden the noise. Was this then a particularly bad case of illness? No, the answer was that the lady at number so and so had just had a baby, four gentlemen had sent straw and the man thought he had better get it all down.

Lady Cardigan was herself ostracised because for years she had lived as a *jeune fille* with Lord Cardigan, more or less openly, before they were able to marry. Once she made a huge ball at Deene Park and not a soul turned up.

She tells a sad story about another friend of hers, Constance de Burgh, which illustrates how ruthless society could be. Constance was married to Lord Ward, who had been considered a *parti* by all the mothers. He had a passion for jewels, buying quantities and lavishing them on his wife who appeared in public flaming with diamonds. He liked best for Constance to put on her jewels when they were alone and would admire her for hours, gazing at her naked body, contrasting the sheen of pearls with that of skin against satin furniture. First she was frightened, then disgusted and appealed to her father. But her parents decided that her husband's pecularities came within the marriage vows and that she must submit. Matters came to a crisis at a ball given by Lady Londonderry. Constance was pregnant, looked delicate and went home early. Lord Ward stayed until three o'clock, and as he approached his house in Park Lane he saw a man leaving. It was Lord Dupplin, an admirer of Constance and a coward, who turned and ran for his life. Lord Ward roused the servants, made them assemble in the hall, then went to his wife's bedroom. 'Get up, madame,' he said, 'my house is yours no longer.' Constance had to dress and in front of the scandalised servants was turned out of the house. She managed to reach her parents' place in Grosvenor Crescent, but they refused to give her shelter and she was obliged to go to her singing master in Conduit Street. From there she went abroad, where her child was prematurely born and she died.

*   *   *

In the second half of the century a number of Americans came to England and had a certain influence on the aristocracy, especially regarding money. At the beginning many Americans, still smarting from the Revolution and the 1815 war, had been decidedly anti-English. Instead they wore gowns designed for the Empress Josephine—and if it were not for their manner of walking Broadway might have been taken for a French street. Not a thing must be English on pain of being stigmatised as *mauvais ton*. To say that someone looked like an Englishman was the cruellest satire that could be uttered.

The English had viewed the Americans with equal distaste. 'I called yesterday in obedience to the Duke of Wellington's entreaties upon Mrs Paterson,'* writes Lady Harriet Granville in 1824. 'She seems a very charming person, very handsome, with *l'air noble* and not a shade of her mother-country. She shook all over when I went into the room, but if for grief at the loss of Mr Paterson . . . or the coldness of the room she received me in, I do not presume to judge.' Paris during the 1820s and '30s had been a whirl of theatres, concerts, drums and junkets. Everything English—except their politics—was now popular and deemed romantic. 'Have I not had another *dîner dansant*,' writes Lady Harriet in 1825, 'and was it not the purtiest thing, as Miss Reynell says, in all Pa-a-ris.'

The French fever lasted until the end of the Second Empire. Crowds of young American girls were brought to buy clothes and be presented—and with luck marry a member of the European aristocracy. The Emperor and Empress liked Americans—the Imperial Balls were sometimes known as *Bals Américains* and the Empress Eugénie even had an American dentist.

Jennie Jerome was taken to Paris with her two sisters in 1867. It was not entirely for pleasure. Her father, Leonard Jerome, was an astonishing man. He had dazzled New York society with his glittering carriages and beautiful horses. He had indulged in fantastic speculations, scandalous love affairs and had given incredible parties. He was passionate about the theatre and above his New York stables, which were furnished with black walnut and carpeted floors, he had built a private stage. Invitations to his first housewarming party had been eagerly sought, two fountains played cologne and champagne, the floral decorations were marvellous and the supper 'cost thousands'. He was in love with Fanny Ronalds, the sensation of New York, who dressed perfectly, entertained on a grand scale, had a wonderful voice, but was unable to demean herself by singing professionally—she could

---

*In 1825 she married Lord Wellesley, while one of her sisters married the 7th Duke of Leeds, and the other Lord Stafford.

however sing in aid of wounded soldiers in Jerome's private theatre. She had given a famous fancy dress ball (cleverly managing to get Jerome, and another lover August Belmont, to pay for it, each unknown to the other). Invitations had been sent out three months in advance so that dresses could be dispatched from Paris. Such hot house fruit, flowers, music, and old wine had never before been seen in Manhattan. Fanny was dressed as Music, in a white satin dress embroidered with bars from Verdi's *Un Ballo in Maschera*, her crown consisted of sparkling quavers and crochets lit up by tiny gas jets concealed in her hair, and her feet were encased in scarlet boots ringed with tiny bells—everyone knew that these were the required gear of prostitutes in John Allen's brothel down the road. Shortly after this she had appeared in a carriage drawn by two showy white horses from Jerome's stable and all New York recognised the gift. Mrs Jerome, who believed that a wife who speaks a cross word loses power over her husband, had announced that she was not feeling too good and must consult a physician in Europe.

Her health recovered splendidly as soon as she reached Paris with her two daughters. Her beauty attracted much attention and she went out a great deal. The court was brilliant, the fêtes gorgeous, the Bois de Boulogne and the Champs-Elysées crowded with splendid equipages. Jennie's sister, Clara, made her debut at one of the Tuileries Balls. She had to walk up the grand staircase in her first low dress between the Cent Gardes in their silver and blue uniforms. When the company was assembled the doors were flung open and their Majesties entered. Eugénie was wearing green velvet with a crown of emeralds and diamonds spiked with pearls. They walked round the circle of bowing and curtseying guests, then proceeded to the ballroom. (At one of the balls an ancient countess was overheard: 'No soup, thank you; a little of that pâté à l'Isthmus de Suez, and truffle à la Harem. Thank you, a little pheasant au bois, a few truffles en serviette—a little of that nice salad à la Paradis, a little pineapple, a few sweet cakes, two glasses of champagne, and a café ice. Nothing more, thank you, I never eat supper.') The Emperor also gave parties at Compiègne, which lasted for several days and consisted of stag hunts, expeditions, entertainments, dances and huge dinners; each evening the guests sat up to a table laden with gold plate.

Clara was much taken up with the subject of clothes: 'In the evening I put on my white with marguerites for the Prince Imperial was to have a Cotillion,' she wrote to her mother from Compiègne. 'We played *chats et souris* so he ran after me and in and out and I finally caught my foot in the Duchesse de Mouchy's dress and fell. I shall need another dress—something

Jennie Jerome as the Empress Theodora at Devonshire House

Jennie promoting Anglo-American relations.

white trimmed with anything you think pretty. I think I must have it. In fact two if possible for these ladies dress so much and never appear in the same . . . P.S. I need a new opera cloak badly—merely something to throw around me at the dinner table.'

With the fall of the Empire several Americans arrived in England with long faces, homesick for Paris. Mrs Jerome was on the whole rather relieved. She did not want Catholic husbands for her daughters and at least now they were in a Protestant country. Clara, who had fallen in love with the Marquis de Tamisier, could only communicate with him by balloon. The Duchesse de Carracciolo and the Comtesse de Bechevet also came to England and took a house in the country, where to the horror of everyone they went shooting dressed in kilts and smoking cigarettes.

Americans seemed almost as outlandish. An American woman was looked upon as a strange abnormal creature with habits and manners something between a Red Indian and a Gaiety Girl. If she talked, dressed, and conducted herself as any normal well-bred lady, everyone, said Jennie Jerome, was astonished. 'I would never have thought *you* were an American'—which was meant to be a compliment. The typical American girl was depicted as beautiful, but dressed in an exaggerated style and speaking—with a nasal twang—the most impossible language. The young lady who, in refusing to eat, says, 'I'm pretty crowded just now', or in explaining why she is travelling alone remarks, 'Poppa don't voyage, he's too fleshy', was thought to represent the national manners. As for American men they were myths, few being idle enough to have time to travel. They were all supposed to be loud and vulgar, as the mothers were unpresentable and the daughters undesirable, unless worth their weight in gold. Years later one lady remarked: 'I like Americans very well, but there are two things I wish they would keep to themselves—their girls and their tinned lobster.'

Mrs Sherwood, who had come to England and encountered what she called 'the choicest specimens of the glorious English women', wrote a cross article called *The English View of Our Society*. 'They do not,' she explained, 'understand our immense distances—especially old ladies who stay at home.' Miss Ricardo, for instance, did not understand; whenever she met a crank she would say, 'So American.' She could not believe there were any servants or good cooking. Mrs Sherwood was indignant when Hamilton Aidé went to New York and never wrote about the lovely breakfasts. 'My dear Mrs Sherwood, we do not come to America to see London and Paris,' Aidé had replied, 'the parties in New York were far more florally magnificent than in London.' He found exaggerated Worth costumes, Francatelli dinners and grandiose hospitality, yet nothing new but replete feeding. At the Queen's Ball in 1886 a number of people stood near Mrs Sherwood and 'commenced commenting' on the politeness of the Prince of Wales to Americans, especially on the fact that he had danced that evening with a young American lady. 'To tell you the truth' said one, 'I do not like all this kow-towing to the Americans . . . and as to seeing them lead off with our Prince, it is shocking to my English heart.' 'But remember,' said another, 'we have married them freely—two duchesses, two countesses and I do not know how many younger sons.' 'Yes,' said the first speaker, who afterwards Mrs Sherwood discovered was the Earl of Sefton, 'they have brought money in where it was needed, that excuses a great deal but it does not excuse the first gentleman in the land from dancing with an American girl at the Queen's Ball'; and he went on to say that he had always admired Labby for his caricatures in *Truth* of the Prince as a cross baby, with a heap of broken toys on a shelf at the top of his head labelled 'American Beauties'.

Once Mrs Sherwood went to an American wedding, celebrated in a pretty little church in the lake district. The bride was very beautiful, lilies-of-the-valley and forget-me-knots were strewn in her path. Afterwards the vicar breakfasted with Mrs Sherwood. 'Why, she is very beautiful and so well-dressed and so is her mother. Are they not unusually refined?' 'No, not *unusually*,' Mrs Sherwood replied crossly. 'I never saw an American before,' the vicar confessed.

Some of Mrs Sherwood's old ladies might have felt their suspicions were well grounded. Most great American fortunes were acquired through such unsavoury means as piracy, slave trading and swindling the Indians. John Jacob Astor, for example, who by 1840 had been the richest man in America, was an uncouth fellow. He ate ice cream and peas with his knife and had been observed wiping his fingers on the sleeve of his dinner neighbour. He had arrived in New York with five dollars, seven flutes and one good suit of clothes, and made his first money by peddling skins and bartering cheap jewellery. In 1786 he had started what was to become the American Fur Company. Huge profits came through selling whisky and rum to the Indians and getting them drunk so they could be swindled over the furs they trapped. He used the money to make himself the largest landowner in the East, evicting farmers, appropriating vast tracts of land and exploiting the workers. He ended up with a stomach disease; able only to ingest milk from a wet nurse and receiving his daily exercise by being tossed about in a blanket—nevertheless up to his last breath he was squeezing arrears from his tenants.

One of poor Mrs Sherwood's complaints was that when Count Boni de Castellane married Anna Gould he went back to Paris and wrote for *Figaro* that Americans—some of them—were very nice people but there was no such thing as Society. Perhaps the trouble was that his father-in-law, Jay Gould, was not accepted. He had started life as a blacksmith and from 1867 onwards had won the reputation of being a financial pirate; for half a century the very name Jay Gould was a by-word for every crime promoted by greed. In any case, whatever Count Boni de Castellane had written, the Americans themselves believed that their society was as fine and rigid as any in Europe. There is a story of a rich Chicago hostess apologising for not being able to send Mr So and So an invitation to her party. 'As you must realise,' she explained to one of her husband's relations, 'he is not of our world.' Her husband's relation agreed, indeed Mr So and So was not of her world, his father was not engaged in the meat canning industry but was merely an English gentleman of ancient lineage.

Each major town had its own Season and its own list. Along the East coast the principal of these were Philadelphia, Richmond, Charleston, Baltimore, Boston and New York. Philadelphia prided itself on having the oldest families in America. Not having an aristocracy meant that to be socially

John Jacob Astor who ate ice cream and peas with his knife.

distinguished you must have ancestors who had lived in America for so many generations—no matter whether they had been criminals or convicts. Thus you might be a son or a daughter of the American Revolution. Better still you might be a Colonial Dame. The Assembly Balls in Philadelphia were a real test of blood. These were grand subscription balls, first given in 1748, and were held twice a year. Guests were culled from the *gratin* of Philadelphian society. There was a long receiving line, consisting of the Social Bride of the Year, the Mother of the Debutante of the Year and other suitable ladies, before whom all guests must bow and curtsey. The Season in any town was run very much on European standards. It lasted from October to May (when there was a rush to resort to the fashionable spots, the cream of which being Newport), and consisted of parties, subscription balls, plays, the opera and all the paraphernalia of calling cards and visits. Young girls were brought out and presented not to the monarch, but to society in general and the eligible bachelors in particular. The wardrobe of a 'young belle' was a major expense. One inventory lists nearly three hundred necessary items costing more than twenty thousand dollars. For a single New York Season the requirements included forty-five gowns, ranging in price from eighty to twenty-five hundred dollars, seven magnificent cloaks, one of which was priced at 450 dollars, and forty-eight chemises of richly embroidered cambric with lace. Among the essential accessories were nine fans, seven jewelled combs, twenty hairnets of gold, silver, pearls and various colours, head ornaments, card cases in gold filigree, gold whist markers and a set of Russian sables and cape, muff and boa.

During the 1850s New York's society had been known as the upper ten thousand. With such numbers it was necessary to appoint an arbiter. Whenever a fashionable hostess planned to give a party she summoned Brown, a fine-looking man with a florid complexion. He inspected her guest list, decided where the musicians were to be placed and in what rooms the supper should be served. As early as 1835 James Gordon Bennett had launched the *New York Herald* realising that mass circulation could be attracted by society gossip, which, under the guise of news, publicised scandal. The newsworthiness of any event was largely determined by money. Money made society go round. The familiar cry came over and over again: 'it must have cost thousands'. Hostesses competed with one another in the lavishness of their entertainments. There had been Mrs Schemmerhorn's famous ball early in 1854. Even the invitation had caused consternation. Everyone must be dressed in Louis XV costume, the mansion would be furnished in authentic style, the servants dressed in the uniforms and wigs of Versailles and a cotillion would be danced lasting two hours. But society had banned costume balls, because fourteen years before, at Henry Brevoort's housewarming party, one young lady had eloped with an impetuous gallant and married before breakfast. Most gentlemen at this time wore facial hair, but whiskers had been forbidden at the court of Louis XV. Did Mrs Schemmerhorn's invitation mean shaving? A scholarly member of the élite saved the day by announcing that all musketeers had been permitted to wear as much hair on their faces as necessary.

Thirty years later Ward McAllister was persuaded that society should be reorganised as a hierarchy with all the eligible marshalled in ascending scale of graded ranks. The foundation was a group known as the patriarchs. There were twenty-nine of these who acted as joint hosts at a series of balls to which each was entitled to bring four ladies and five gentlemen. Success was largely due to the difficulty of securing invitations. The patriarchs were charged not only with the duty of leading society but of creating it as well. The schedule was devised, as methodically as a timetable, by McAllister and Mrs Astor. On Monday and Friday nights those who had boxes at the Academy of Music attended the opera, arriving at the end of the first act, then on Monday nights they would go to the Patriarch Balls, Assembly Balls and Family Circle Dancing classes—all held at Delmonico's. On the third Monday in January was Mrs Astor's annual ball—the most sacred ceremony of the year. Banks of flowers adorned the house, precious antique lace draped the hostess's shoulders and edged her huge puffed sleeves and pointed bodice. She wore a long train of dark velvet, a skirt of satin, embroidered with pearls, silver and gold; she glittered with diamonds. Every week she gave a dinner party to which only the topmost rung of the hierarchy was invited. The table was illuminated by gold candelabra and decorated by masses of flowers, a gold service was used. The guests must be seated by eight o'clock. Gastronomy was a holy discipline. It was unlikely that you would meet an idea at Mrs Astor's table, yet some of the hierarchy had a wistful reverence for intellectual life. The sacred 400—to whit those who had received invitations for Mrs Astor's ball in 1892—was a substitute for an aristocracy and court, just as Mrs Astor was a substitute for the Queen.

It was a position she had worked hard to gain. First there had been a spending competition to establish who, between Mary, wife of William Waldorf (later Baron Astor of Hever), and herself, Caroline, wife of John Jacob IV, was *the* Mrs Astor. She had won and it was *her* comments, *her* parties, and the state of *her* jewellery that was reported in the press.

Another orgy of spending had been enjoyed by the Vanderbilts (whose money had been made in railways by old Commodore Vanderbilt who, like Jay Gould, was not received in society, his language keeping him beyond the

An American Ball and its Belle.

The Breakers, Newport, Alice Vanderbilt's country house.

pale). Two monuments in Newport had been erected to the struggle of becoming *the* Mrs Vanderbilt. The Breakers was said to have cost ten million dollars and was built by Cornelius for his wife Alice—it had seventy rooms designed round a baronial hall rising more than forty-five feet through two floors, a front door that weighed seventy tons, fresh salt water piped into the bathrooms and a billiard room that was green marble from top to bottom. Marble House, which cost a mere two million dollars, was built by William for Alva, being modelled on the Temple of the Sun at Baalbek with a driveway of white marble. Alva augmented this in 1883 by giving a fancy dress ball, an extravaganza costing 250,000 dollars. One of the guests, Henry Clews, reported: 'The ball seemed to have the effect of levelling up among the social ranks of upper tendom, and placing the Vanderbilts at the top of the heap in what is recognised as good society in New York. So far as cost, richness of costume and newspaper celebrity were concerned that ball had, perhaps, no equal in history. It may not have been quite so expensive as the feast of Alexander the Great at Babylon, some of the entertainments of Cleopatra to Augustus and Mark Antony, or a few of the magnificent

Alva Vanderbilt ready for her ball.

banquets of Louis XIV, but when viewed from every essential standpoint, and taking into account our advanced civilisation, I have no hesitation in saying that the Vanderbilt ball was superior to any of those grand historic displays of festivity and amusement.'

The *New York Sun* added: 'In lavishness of expenditure and brilliancy of dress, it far out did any ball ever given in this city. It was a scene from Faery Land, Mother Goose, the Picture Galleries, the Courts and Camps of Europe, Audubon's Birds of America, Heathen Myths and Christian Legends . . .'

Rivalry was not only inter-family. There was hot competition for social leadership within the 400. Hostesses competed with their food, wine, dances and balls. 'I know of no profession, art, or trade that women are working in today, as taxing on mental resources as being a leader of society,' Mrs Oliver Hazard Belmont sighed. Mrs Stuyvesant Fish's parties were designed to be unforgettable. She abhorred dullness, against which she embarked on a crusade. One night in her ballroom a troupe from the circus performed and a baby elephant passed round the peanuts. Another time, boys, dressed as cats, distributed live white mice among the guests. She gave a party for dolls, at which all the guests spoke in baby talk, and a banquet for a hundred dogs, which were all decorated in diamonds, with a small monkey sitting in the place usually reserved for Mrs Astor. 'We are not rich. We have only a few million,' Mrs Fish has been quoted as saying. One of the most tiresome problems was how best to set off one's jewels. Mrs Dexel had her pearls re-set in a wide band which belted her waist, diagonally crossed her bosom and shoulder and descended her back. Mrs Frederick Vanderbilt wore a single jewel dangling round her feet and would progress to her box at the opera kicking a great uncut ruby or sapphire, which was attached to her waist by a rope of pearls. Another lady had a high chair built for her so that her glittering torso could be visible to everyone.

The 1890s were remarkable for America in the record of unpublished exports: heiresses. The total value in dollars was far above the combined total of wheat, corn, cattle and other food stuffs. One theory was that as a revenue producer for the Empire, Britain's titled nobility raised more money than any other scheme yet devised, and Republican France held on to her obsolete titles largely for the same reason. 'How I should hate to be May Goelet,' wrote Daisy, Princess of Pless, 'all those odious little Frenchmen, and dozens of others crowding round her millions. An English Duke does not *crowd around*—he merely accepts a millionairess.' May Goelet was soon merely accepted by the Duke of Roxburghe.

Often the American heiresses—and their fathers—received rather raw deals. Helena Zimmerman eloped with the Duke of Manchester (Louisa's

Mrs Stuyvesant Fish whose parties were designed to be unforgettable.

An unpublished American export—the millionairess May Goelet, who married the Duke of Roxburghe.

son), who was notoriously dissipated and had just been faced with bankruptcy, and her father, who was a Cincinnati iron and oil millionaire, had to keep paying all the Duke's entertainment and travel bills. Alice Thaw, a railway heiress from Pittsburgh, married the impecunious Earl of Yarmouth, who had chased her all over America, and the couple left for England pursued by creditors eager to appropriate the Earl's luggage. In 1888 the 8th Duke of Marlborough had arrived in New York (hot from a scandal involving Lady Aylesford) with brand-new baggage, seeking gold. Everything about 'his Grace of Marlborough' was clean except for his reputation, remarked the press: he was 'badness personified'. Nevertheless he managed to catch Lily Hammersley, who had changed her name from Lillian because it rhymed with million, and who, according to the press, was a common-looking lady with a moustache and an annual income of 150,000 dollars, which allowed her to feed her spaniels on fricassée of chicken, cream and macaroons. On reaching England the Duchess found that, owing to the Duke's divorce, Queen Victoria would not receive her at court and that her husband topped the list of lovers of the well-known houri Lady Colin Campbell, to whom he had given a palace in Venice. Still, she valiantly furnished Blenheim with a new lead roof and an organ; three years later the Duke died in his laboratory. Three years later again the new Duke married Consuelo Vanderbilt. It has been suggested that the match was yet another move in Alva's campaign to become *the* Mrs Vanderbilt. Both she and Alice had teenage daughters about to make their debuts, and marriage to the Duke of Marlborough was checkmate. In 1920, when Consuelo was divorced, she was depicted as an agonised weeping girl who had been sold by her mother— she had tried to elope with a young society bachelor, Winthrop Rutherford, but her mother kept her prisoner in a guarded room threatening to have a heart attack. The dowry, it was said, was 2,500,000 dollars, money which was used to renovate Blenheim.

Many Americans puritanically disapproved of the European aristocrat's habit of looking for heiresses rather than opportunities for his earning money. Leonard Jerome, who outwardly seemed so aristocratic, certainly felt this, but his wife caught the *parti* fever. To secure a good match for one's daughters required a great deal of energy: between them Lord Ernest Hamilton's seven sisters managed to marry two dukes, one marquis and four earls; Lord Randolph Churchill's five sisters caught five eldest sons, four of whom were peers, while Louisa, Duchess of Manchester's daughters married, as she dictated, one duke and two earls. One lady told Anita Leslie that she had accepted a proposal just to get away from her mother who kept telling her not to sit with her legs crossed. However, on the whole, it was quite difficult for a girl to get married at all.

'I never thought it was a good match in money point of view,' Jennie wrote to her mother, on the subject of her youngest sister. 'There are so few *partis* and when I see a girl like Georgie with everything that money, dress and position can do for her hanging on year after year, and she is not the only one—there is one of the Duchess of Newcastle's daughters, Lady Beatrix Clinton, a nice looking girl, very well educated with a large fortune, they say £12,000 a year, well this is her first season and she insists on marrying Johnny Kaye's brother, Mr Cecil Kaye, a sick tiresome youth . . .'

The Jerome sisters, when they arrived in England with their Paris dresses, thought themselves far superior to English girls. When Jennie went to Blenheim she discovered she worked harder at music, was more fluent in French and German, was better read and a better rider than her husband's sisters. (Poor Rosamund was being dragged through the Season with a liver complaint and was being scolded by the Duchess of Marlborough for looking plain, although eventually she was successfully married to Lord de Ramsey.)

Jennie wrote letters to her mother laughing at their frumpy clothes, the water jugs on the dining table and the thick tumblers. They knew nothing about Paris fashions and the table mats were the wrong shape. When Clara went to stay she annoyed everybody by talking about the Château de Compiègne rather than admiring Blenheim.

She was still obsessed by clothes, especially the Ascot fashions. 'We have just come home and I sit down immediately and write you with my hat on,' she wrote to her mother, 'we were a cheery party . . . I never saw such wonderful *toilettes* and the Royal Enclosure was very swell and select. Lord Harrington took me to lunch in a private room with the royalties, the Prince himself giving his arm to Jennie and altogether the day was *très réussi*. Thursday was Gold Cup Day. Jennie wore her wedding dress with new crêpe de chine trimmings and I my pale blue with marguerites *au corsage* and my new marguerite bonnet which is very pretty. We managed to have lots of fun after the races as Oliver Montagu invited us to have tea at the barracks of the Blues at Windsor. So we all crowded on top of the coach and Oliver and Colonel Williams received us in grand scale with tea on the lawn the band playing . . .'

Another unpublished export: Consuelo Vanderbilt,
forced into marriage with the Duke of Marlborough.

Chapter 9

LONDON society remained closed until the 1890s. Then, as Lady St Helier said, of a sudden the conventional rules were swept away and those who had the courage and appreciation to open their houses to everyone who was interesting and distinguished found an ideally delightful society waiting. The old-fashioned did not like it at all. To have a good cook, to be the smartest dressed woman, to give magnificent entertainments where a fortune was spent on flowers and decorations, to be the favoured guest of royalty, to have sailed on the wind of social disaster without being shipwrecked, these seemed to be a few of the targets some of the smartest people in London society were aiming for. It was all very fast and all very *American*. It was all part of a change from an aristocracy to a plutocracy. 'Your society now reminds me of the dishes served in restaurants,' 'Marmaduke' wrote in *Truth* in 1904, 'the new material is abominable but it is arranged with rich-coloured sauces which make it look especially excellent. In the West End streets, drawing rooms and theatres I meet men and women who are faultlessly dressed, but there is an obvious absence of distinction about them, their manners are distressing and their conversation shows that they never received a first-class education. The magnificent carriages, the precious gems and exquisite dresses seem to have been assumed by those for whom they were not originally provided. The test of the intellectual condition of a nation is its conversation ... There is never a trace of intelligence or originality, and if there were it would be instantly discouraged for the brains of most of your West End men and women of today could not endure the strain. But talk of money and in an instant every face lights up, an eager look comes into the eyes . . .'

Not all levels accepted change. The Prince of Wales himself was easy-going and available to all sorts of people who hitherto would have sought his acquaintance in vain. But the Marlborough House Set itself was not at all interested in any 'ideally delightful' society that might be waiting.

'We did not like brains,' Lady Warwick wrote. 'As for money our only understanding lay in the spending not in the making of it.' Artists, writers, musicians and lawyers might disturb, over-stimulate or even bore. 'We considered the heads of historic houses who read serious works, encouraged scientists and the like, very, very dull.' Lady Warwick was, as Anita Leslie says, a typical Edwardian. She was beautiful, she was an heiress and she spent her fortune on entertaining the Prince of Wales, at one stage building a special railway station for him at Easton. 'I have never seen one who was so completely fascinating as Daisy Brooke,' Elinor Glyn wrote. 'She would sail in . . . carrying her piping bull-finch, her lovely eyes smiling with the merry innocent expression of a Persian kitten . . .' When she came out many balls were given in her honour (in her day men also gave balls and those given by the Life Guards or the Blues were especially celebrated for their excellent dancing). She was fêted, feasted, courted and adored, spinning in a continual round of gaieties, floating to rhythmic waltzes in diaphanous tulles and chiffons. And then next day she would repair to that select spot in Hyde Park between Albert and Grosvenor Gates where the small circle of society met on its morning rides and drives. One would book friends for lunch perhaps, drive one's phaeton with high-stepping chestnuts, browns and bays down Piccadilly, prancing on the wide sweep of the pavement, glancing up at the Turf Club window as a possible place to find an extra man for a dinner party.

Off they would go to fancy dress balls at Stafford House and Warwick Castle. The railway platform would be piled with mountains of roofed boxes, for changing was an occupation which occurred at least four times a day. Tactful hostesses took trouble with allocating rooms, but there were still misadventures. Lord Charles Beresford once tiptoed into a dark room and jumped into the middle of what he thought was Lady Warwick's bed shouting cock-a-doodle-doo, to find himself between the startled Bishop of Chester and his wife.

Lady Warwick says that every extravagance of her small group was eagerly followed up in almost every paper as a proper expenditure of money. It was good for trade. 'This strengthened the position of our circle because it made us a privileged class.' Their patronage was sought by tradesmen, eager to gratify their every caprice for the honour of serving them, while waiting indefinitely for their money. In those days, bills were presented yearly. In London during the Season the Marlborough House Set turned night into day. They would dine long and late, trifle with the opera for an hour or so, or watch the ballet. To keep going in the Prince of Wales's set required an enormous outlay. The extravagance involved—especially in those huge country houses—was so considerable that several of Prince Edward's friends could not afford it. In some houses the royal suite would be specially refurnished for each visit and the ordinary cook would be replaced by a specialist whose skill was only equalled by his wastefulness. People had been known to economise for a whole year so that they could entertain royalty for one weekend. Two benefactors called Lewis were a great standby. The whole *jeunesse dorée* of the eighties and nineties were forever flying to one or the other. One was Samuel Lewis the moneylender—some people owed him thousands. The other was the lawyer George Lewis, who settled hundreds of society cases out of court.

Lady Warwick ended up disillusioned with the social scene: 'All these silly women, Gladys [de Grey] and Rachel and Georgie [Countess Howe] all thinking life is bounded on one side by Worth and Cartier and on the other by King Edward's court and bridge . . . I am going to get back to work, or at least as much as I can do with the d—d London Season to tackle as well!!'

Queen Victoria died in 1901. King Edward's coronation went off splendidly, apart from poor Louisa (now Duchess of Devonshire), who after the long ceremony hurried off to the Ladies in the wake of the royal procession, but found herself stopped by a line of Grenadier Guards. Jennie Churchill, who was descending from the King's special box, heard her upbraiding all the other peeresses, many of whom were themselves uncomfortable; trying to push her way past she missed her footing and fell headlong down a flight of steps, landing at the feet of the Chancellor of the Exchequer.

Neither before nor after his coronation did Edward make any secret of his affairs. He chose mature ladies, hung with their own family jewels. Alice Keppel was ideal for him. Her daughters were taught to call him Kingy and he allowed them to race bread and butter up and down his trouser legs. Her husband was often heard muttering darkly about financial crises, but luckily Mrs Keppel was irresistible to bank managers. She would sweep in, place her parasol on the table, then slowly lift her veil. The bank manager would catch his breath, her request would be granted and out she would sweep again leaving behind her own special fragrance of spring blossom and fresh green sap. During the last years of his life, Edward had also another mistress. Agnes Keyser was calm and sympathetic and gave him a sense of security. She tried to discipline his eating habits and instead of stuffing him with too much rich

Daisy, Countess of Warwick, as Queen of Assyria.

That select spot in Hyde Park
where everyone met.

Alice Keppel, irresistible to bank managers.

food and drink as all other hostesses did, she struggled to reduce his diet to healthy nursery fare. Healthy fare or not, he died in 1910 and every social event of the Season had to be cancelled.

In 1911 Lady Diana Manners (afterwards Lady Diana Cooper) was presented to King George V and Queen Mary. She had made her own train, she says, three yards of cream net sprinkled generously with pink rose-petals, each attached by a diamond dew-drop. By now there were special parties for young people, known as *Bals Blancs*, sometimes there were three or four a night. Young girls, shy, raw, deplorably dressed with wispy shapeless hair and gloves drawn above their elbows danced under the crude glare of the electric light—which did nothing for beauties either and robbed jewels of their smoulder.

There were still balls at Londonderry, Bridgewater and Stafford Houses, and the Duke of Sutherland could still pin £1,000 in notes on his wife's pillow, but he was the first rich man to sense that the social revolution would undermine his fortune and Stafford House in 1912 was the first great London house to be sold. Lloyd George, the Chancellor of the Exchequer, loathed the privileged rich and his 1909 budget had attacked landowners, peerage and crown—he himself however sold honours, at anything from £6,000 for a knighthood to £150,000 for a peerage, and put the proceeds into the Liberal Party. The new income tax was an irritating complication. Lady Diana Cooper remembers when it rose to eleven pence in the pound and they all thought her father, who was always threatening bankruptcy, was going to die, he looked so white.

Society had ceased to be a force in politics and was merely a force in the retail trade. Society was for society's sake, and to use a vulgar expression Lady Dorothy Nevill lamented, it was on the make. 'What is the life of a rich man today? A sort of firework?' The whole standard of living had changed during her lifetime, the bustle of the Stock Exchange had been imported into the drawing rooms of Mayfair. Mere wealth seemed a passport to open most doors, etiquette was lax and the young were going berserk.

Lady Diana Cooper was always being criticised, she says, for her behaviour. Another attempt was made to revive the Eglinton tournament, which took place at Earl's Court with tickets costing £20 each. Lady Curzon was Queen of Beauty and Lady Diana was a lady of her court. She did not care for her horse, which was an ordinary looking fellow borrowed from the Household Cavalry, nor did she care for the boring Elizabethan dress she was supposed to be wearing. So she hired Richard II's stage horse, which had a

OVERLEAF: Edward, Prince of Wales, arriving at Ascot.

Lady Diana Cooper as Britannia.

Nancy Cunard and Lady Diana Cooper with two
friends at a musical tableau at the French Embassy,
June 1914.

mane and tail down to the ground, and designed for herself a black velvet
Holbein dress, which had nothing to do with the tournament, and rode
round with Prince Felix Youssupoff who was mounted equally unsuitably on
a white Arab and dressed in his Russian clothes. 'Of course they were cross
with us for cheating and another score was marked up against us,' writes
Lady Diana. Undaunted they dashed on, to Venice for example, to climb the
striped gondola poles and dive into the dark canals, mad exploits done for
love—she knew one man who had eaten a centipede to please his young lady.
There was a disastrous party on board a boat on the Thames with dancing to a
quartet from Thomas Beecham's orchestra. Even before they sailed Denis
Anson was swinging from the rigging. After supper Anson and a member of
the quartet dived overboard—never to be seen again. The Great War was
upon them, Denis Anson would surely have been the first to be killed, while
the musician was consumptive and due to die anyway, but this was a
shattering end to the carefree life that Lady Diana knew. It was July, and
August 1914 was very near.

Chapter 10

TRUE to tradition the army was still the preserve of the aristocracy. Fighting was a gentleman's profession. The Great War demolished not only the flower of the aristocracy but much class distinction. Afterwards nothing was ever the same again. With their fathers and sons killed, many families were short of money. Some of the older aristocracy, pressed by income tax, sold their London houses and retired to the country. It was not only income tax but lack of staff. Women who had been earning high wages making munitions were not interested in kitchens or housekeeper's cupboards, while men who had survived the trenches were not keen on serving in pantries and at table. Coal fires were changing to electricity, mansions to mansion flats, balls to cocktail parties, actors and actresses were trying to be ladies and gentlemen and ladies and gentlemen were trying to be actors and actresses, peers were becoming socialists and socialists were becoming peers. As one aristocratic lady said: 'The bottom is coming up, my dear, and the top's coming down.' Democracy ate steadily into the House of Lords. In 1923 Stanley Baldwin was chosen to be prime minister, rather than Lord Curzon. The King realised that a prime minister in the House of Lords would be unacceptable to the new Labour members in the House of Commons.

George V's court was a model of decency and sobriety. The King, like Queen Victoria, did not care for the society of fast and fashionable people. He did not care either for entertaining and preferred to dine alone with the Queen and pore over his stamp collection until 10.15 when it was time for bed. Relations with his sons were none too good. They found it boring at home, preferring to go off to night clubs and dance. Yet again the Prince of Wales and his friends were the pace-setters. To defy the old order of society it was necessary to do something outrageous. Mrs Dudley Ward appeared one night at the Embassy Club in a backless evening dress worn with a long scarf, a spray of expensive artificial flowers on the shoulder and five or six bracelets encircling her bare arms. Before long every young woman was cutting her hair short and trying to look as slender as an adolescent boy, they sat chain smoking, drinking cocktails and wearing *make-up*. It was deeply shocking to the older generation. 'Fashionable women of a certain class are rapidly returning to barbarism,' declared Viscountess Templeton in the *Weekly Dispatch*, and she quoted an officer who said he could not dance at the Victory Ball because he was not able to ask any of the women—they did not have enough clothes on.

Next, society ladies started going into trade. Mrs Dudley Coats opened a shop specialising in scent and wedding clothes, called 'Audrey'. Poppy Baring opened 'Poppy', a dress shop, and Barbara Cartland had a hat shop—called 'Barbara'—which was not a success as every time a customer called the proprietor was out to lunch wearing the hats. Barbara Cartland's great-aunts thought her very fast. She wore face powder, painted her lips and wrote a novel in which the Duke, on page 200, kissed the heroine, rather chastely. The great-aunts said it proved what they had always suspected, that she was immoral and must have written from experience. Certainly she was romantic. She and her friends danced all night—and some of the day as well. As soon as they arrived in the country for a hunt ball they would start. There were afternoon dances and *thé dansants*. In her memories the sky was bright with stars, the moon was full and she received forty-nine proposals before she said yes.

Men who loved her would stand outside her house late at night, in a silent salute. Others who had dropped her home in the early hours of the morning would leave a note and a bunch of flowers a few hours later for her to find on her breakfast tray: 'Good morning, darling—I want these roses to see you . . .' What no historian seems to have recorded, she explains, was the mental state of those men returning from the trenches. To them, she and her contemporaries were everything they thought they would never see again. They wanted to get married, she says, they wanted love. One of the most popular places to dance was the Grafton Galleries—an enormous picture gallery which was so respectable that when there were exhibitions of nude drawings they were covered at night by pieces of tissue paper. Only non-alcoholic drinks were served, iced coffee and a concoction known as Turk's Blood—a bright pink beverage in which floated small cubes of unidentified fruit. One ate sandwiches and iced cakes and danced to a negro band. Or there was Rectors, deep underground in a cellar in Tottenham Court Road,

Barbara Cartland, who once had a hat shop.

the first place to have face powder, chalk-white, free in the ladies' lavatory.

When they were not dancing, the 'Bright Young People' were busy with all sorts of other activities. There were treasure hunts and hoaxes. Theresa Jungman masqueraded as a Russian Princess and arrived at a garden party with a borzoi and a casket of jewels that she said she had saved from the Bolshevik revolution. Brian Howard posed as a painter, Bruno Hat, and gave an exhibition of paintings, some of them executed on cork bath-mats. A lecture was given by a 'well-known German psychologist' which deeply impressed many distinguished professors and heads of colleges—it turned out to be a parody using all the jargon that psychologists use without one word of meaning.

People arrived at a Baby Party with their reluctant old nannies and rode donkeys round Rutland Gate. Norman Hartnell gave a Circus party, complete with performing wolves, acrobats and Eleanor Smith who arrived up the steps on a white pony with a scarlet saddle. Brian Howard and Elizabeth Ponsonby gave a Bath and Bottle party at St George's Swimming Baths which was widely reported in the press and shocked a lot of people. Tom Driberg, the originator of the William Hickey column, was there and had to keep on rushing out to the nearest telephone kiosk to keep his editors up to date with the latest scandal. Bathing dresses were of the most dazzling kinds, the guests danced to a negro band, rubber horses and flowers floated in the water, which was illuminated by coloured spot-lights, and a special Bathwater Cocktail was served in the gallery. Eventually the police arrived to encourage the guests to leave and were dragged off by the more rapacious into changing-room cubicles.

Sometimes there were so many fancy dress parties that Cecil Beaton said it was quite usual for him never to put on ordinary clothes for a week or ten days at a stretch. Brian Howard loved dressing up. He appeared at one party dressed as a duchess of 1905: 'Let me describe my toilette . . . Poised on the largest nut-brown wig in the world I wore a colossal grey velvet hat, embellished with a cascade of grey ostrich plumes, and seven magenta cabbage roses. Round my neck there was a diamond and pearl dog collar; a lorgnette on the end of a black ribbon, and a narrow black boa. The dress of grey gauze, tight at the waist, and with a slight trim; the corsage was decorated in front with a fichu of lace, and upon this I pinned two monstrous cameos, and a butterfly made of diamonds. On the long trailing skirt there were oblong insertions of lace. Besides this I wore black gloves which went above the elbows; black silk stockings, gartered in pink, and extremely high-heeled patent leather shoes. We had arrived at the Harry Browns earlier in the evening and created such furore that we had had to leave.' No one had seen a fancy dress of that period before and also there was the question of his face. Willie Clarkson had taken an hour to make him up: 'my dear, in his hands my face suddenly became that of some bastard daughter with a dozen mothers.'

After the war, publicity for society ladies had revived. One of the reasons Edwardian affairs lasted so long may have been because columnists did not exist. Occasionally resentful servants wrote a little scandal for *Titbits* but such fabrications were not taken seriously. The older generation disapproved of journalism and believed that a lady's name should appear in the newspapers only on four occasions—her birth, her marriage, the birth of her children and her death. But, after the war, newspapers imported society people to write society news—Viscount Castlerosse, the Marquis of Donegal and Tom Driberg were three—and their columns reflected a society which had its being virtually only within the limits of the public imagination. What the press described as society was society.

In time, every daily newspaper was running a gossip column so that during the twenties and thirties parties were no longer mere exchanges of hospitality, but also public spectacles. When Barbara Cartland began to be mentioned in gossip columns everyone went round asking how much she paid to get in.

There was a great deal of American-style rivalry between the hostesses— indeed many of the hostesses *were* American. They vied with each other to capture the Prince of Wales as the star turn of their entertainments and measured their success by the length of time he stayed dancing in their ballrooms or sitting with a girl in their supper rooms. The idea was that every hostess must mix her guests, showing off the celebrities that she had managed to catch, rather like butterfly specimens. Each had her own speciality.

Lady Cunard patronised the arts. At the beginning of her entertaining career she had been rebuffed by the more old-fashioned members of society, but by 1907 she was well-established—Maurice Baring was able to say that he could resign honourably from the Society for Prevention of Cruelty to Lady Cunard. Her luncheon and dinner parties were served at a circular table of lapis lazuli. Her one great disappointment was her daughter Nancy with whom she had hoped to make a big splash during the Season. Nancy however preferred leopard-skins, turbans, the Eiffel Tower Restaurant and the Café Royal to frilly dresses, picture hats and the social programme her mother prepared—the last straw was her black lover.

The Hon. Mrs Greville was richer than Lady Cunard and made no secret that her money came from beer. She referred to Lady Cunard as the Yellow

Brian Howard, another who loved dressing up.

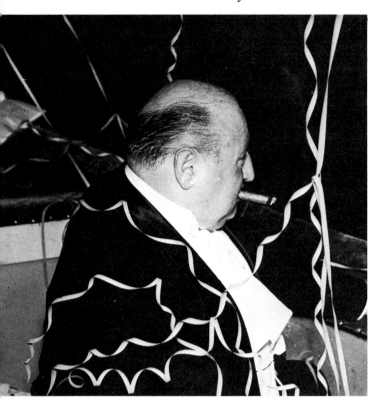

Viscount Castlerosse.

Canary, and sometimes the Lollipop, and was most irritated by the frequent presence of the Prince of Wales and the Duke of Kent at the lapis lazuli dinner table—Mrs Greville specialised in royalty and the higher peerage. Lady Colefax liked artists and intellectuals. She gave parties meticulously constructed round celebrities in her house in Chelsea, which was restfully decorated in pale almond greens and greys and brightened with touches of yellow and rechristened by Osbert Sitwell 'Lion's Corner House'. Beverley Nichols recalls her neighbour, Syrie Maugham, making him climb on a wheelbarrow to look over the wall and see whether she had managed to get Charlie Chaplin for lunch. At weekends Lady Colefax would spend all morning writing invitations on postcards. Sometimes guests might receive three or four of these all at once, each for a separate occasion. Lord Berners adapted a Victorian toy, so that when the button was pressed a large black head opened its mouth and spewed out a stream of her invitations.

Perhaps Mrs Laura Corrigan was the most eccentric American hostess of all. She was supposed to have started life as a telephone operator and have

Emerald Cunard, who served dinner at a table of lapis lazuli.

made a blind date with a multi-millionaire steel magnate, getting him to the altar next morning. She was presented at court by the American Ambassadress and took Mrs Keppel's house in Grosvenor Square together with (for a certain sum) Mrs Keppel's guest list. Invitations to her first party were declined. Who *was* Mrs Corrigan? So she hired a secretary who had worked for Lady Londonderry and on the invitation cards for her next party she announced that there would be a cabaret from Paris and a tombola. Guests received gold cigarette cases from Cartier's, coroneted gold sock suspenders, initialled braces with gold tabs, gold bags and tortoiseshell steel combs inlaid with gold. Soon people began to agree that Mrs Corrigan was rather amusing and as for her malapropisms they were famous. Mrs Keppel's house she called her *ventre à terre*, some cathedral she visited had magnificent flying buttocks and, when asked if she knew the Dardanelles, she replied: 'Wal, no, but I've got lots of letters of introduction to them. I guess they're *terribly* nice people.'

Her auburn wigs were well-known. She owned several, which travelled

Nancy Cunard—the last straw was her black lover.

The eccentric Laura Corrigan—a wig for all seasons.

round in a box known as Laura's wigwam, and were dressed for every occasion: *bien coiffé* for luncheon, *bouffant* for balls, one slightly rumpled for breakfast in bed, another wind-blown for walks in the country, and one dishevelled for a visit to the hairdresser—she carried out an elaborate fiction that her hair was real. For bathing she had a wig with a cap attached. Once it came off in Lord Dudley's swimming pool and she was under the water for quite some time retrieving it. Then she went indoors as if nothing had happened and appeared half an hour late for dinner explaining that she had been drying her hair. She was just the kind of rich outsider that post-war society was willing to accept. In 1931 she rented the Palazzo Mocenigo in Venice and in every room there were notices telling her guests not to tip the servants, never to buy stamps or cigarettes and not to pay for their washing, cleaning or any drinks they consumed at the Grand Hotel or the Lido.

Lady Londonderry (wife of the 7th marquis) had a snake tatooed on her ankle and kept up the family tradition by being one of the most celebrated and frightening hostesses of her time. Hazel Lavery says that shortly after her husband, the portrait painter, had been knighted, she was so overcome with fright at one of Lady Londonderry's receptions that she could only murmur her name to the man: 'At the bottom of the staircase, m'lady, and through the baize door,' he whispered in reply.

Although there were still a number of private houses in which the hostess received her friends—'at home' in the real sense—one by one the big mansions like Devonshire House and Grosvenor House were giving way to blocks of flats or hotels, and many entertainments, especially debutante balls were now lavish and anonymous. Queen Charlotte's was one of the charity balls that were accepted as regular seasonal events. Cartloads of flowers came from the florist, a band from the band agency and invitations were sent to hundreds of more or less unknown guests. In 1928 Lady Ellesmere gave a ball at Bridgewater House and a major gate-crashing scandal ensued. There were 300 guests whom Lady Ellesmere did not recognise and who were thrown out—with Cecil Beaton among them. Everybody gave interviews to the press. Lord and Lady Ellesmere had plenty to say, so did the guests who had been turned out, together with their brothers and mothers and the other uninvited guests who had not been turned out. Anyone in the social world who felt they had something to say joined in. The gatecrashers argued that entertaining had grown so informal that it was now usual to take along a few friends to all social functions. Lady Ellesmere complained that she had discovered a young man at the ball who had brought his wife with him when she had invited him as a bachelor.

'To all young men in London of passable parentage, manners and appearance, with enough money . . . the uninvited or unwanted hostess has become an increasing problem,' Lord Castlerosse commented in the *Sunday Express.* 'A week never passes but I receive several of those familiar envelopes containing an important card which announces to me that some lady with a reasonable name will be at home to me. In nine cases out of ten I do not know her, and I do not want to know her, and yet she asks me, more she demands an answer, without doing one the courtesy of enclosing the usual stamped and addressed envelope. At the height of the season the mere expense of postage becomes intolerable . . .'

The introduction of daughters to the marriage market had become the principal object of formal entertaining. Debutantes were news. Margaret Whigham (afterwards Duchess of Argyll) was Deb of the Year in 1930. The climate in which she came out, she says, was strictly moral, largely because of the stormy reaction against the fast 'hard drinking decadence of the '20s'. During her first Season she was never allowed out unless accompanied by her nanny. Until 1930, she says, a debutante would have been a person from whom any man over the age of twenty-six would have run a mile—a painfully shy mouse, lacking in make-up and conversation. But the girls of 1930 were not only good-looking, they knew how to dress and they had self-confidence. All at once the well-known married beauties began to feel threatened by the young girl. Newspapers featured debutantes who had

The frightening Lady
Londonderry.

become front-page news along with royalty, politicians and actresses.
According to the *Bystander* Margaret Whigham was 'quite the smartest jeune
fille' London had seen for a long time. And according to Barbara Cartland,
who drips a suspicion of cider vinegar into her honeyed words, Margaret
Whigham organised all her own publicity—she was charming to journalists
and gave what we should call press conferences, in consequence she had far
better and more flattering press coverage than any film star.

Margaret Whigham says that she was brought out in London rather than
New York because Prohibition was on and her mother was appalled to see
young girls in the cloakrooms at New York debutante balls dead drunk from
what they called moonshine, a lethal concoction of raw spirits. So it was
announced in *The Times*: that Mr and Mrs George Hay Whigham had arrived
at 6 Audley Square, which they had rented for the Season. She tells us that
not wanting to waste a minute they planned her coming out dance for May 1.
It was a calculated risk, since it was possible that once all the debutantes had
been to her dance their mothers might not bother to invite her to theirs. In

those days the build-up for a debutante's coming out was really exciting, she says. She was allowed to order a dozen beautiful dresses and many day outfits ('awful word!') for the Derby, Ascot and the many lunch parties to which she anticipated being invited. 'Forget-me-not blue will form the very lovely frock of tonight's blue-bred debutante Miss Margaret Whigham,' reported the *Daily Telegraph*. Audley Square was filled with spring flowers and wearing a turquoise embroidered tulle dress she received the guests (many of whom, like Lady Ellesmere, she can never have set eyes upon) while Ambrose played sweet music. She was surprised and flattered from that night on to find herself prominently featured in the social columns. Every night there was a ball or reception. But the young ladies were again in the grip of chaperones. Before each dance the mother of a debutante would give a dinner party of young people after which the other mothers would go to the dance and spend the evening sitting on gold chairs. 'My mother and I' soon decided that this routine was not for them; if Margaret promised to go home, driven by the chauffeur, her mother agreed to make a brief appearance and then vanish. There were still dance programmes, the worst that could happen to any girl was for her programme to be unfilled. To combat this Margaret devised the Whigham system. For the first half-hour she agreed to dance with any boy who asked her, however dim. Then, as her favourite beaux appeared, she would ruthlessly fill up her programme all over again.

Three weeks after her dance she was presented—schooled in her court curtsey by Madame Vacani, the ultimate authority. She found it quite breathtaking, remembering that she wore white tulle embroidered with silver and pearls, while the Queen was in gold brocade, emeralds and diamonds. She recalled the magnificent state rooms, the gold and scarlet ballroom blazing with orders, decorations, swords and coloured tunics: 'an unforgettable sight.' The year rushed by: the Derby with Aly Khan, dancing in the Embassy, charity matinees—'a whirl through wonderland' is how she describes it. Her energy was boundless. She would have dinner with one man, go home at 10.30, and sally out to meet another at the Embassy or the Café de Paris, floating on again to the Florida or the Silver Slipper.

When Britain went off the gold standard in October 1931, the *Daily Express* remarked: 'As an example to the girlhood of Britain, the lovely Margaret Whigham has decided, in the interests of economy, to have her hair re-set only once a fortnight in future, and to stop wearing stockings in the evenings. On the other hand to stimulate trade she has bought four new evening dresses.' This provoked what Margaret Whigham calls some 'not so good-natured fun'. The *Daily Worker* said: 'This should be a lesson to the wives of the unemployed, whose extravagant habits include setting their

Margaret Whigham and Charles Sweeny.

hair in curl-papers every day and buying no dresses at all.'

Margaret Whigham's debut concluded in 1933 with jilting the Earl of Warwick, marrying Charles Sweeny and being serenaded by Cole Porter:

> You're the nimble tread of the feet of Fred Astaire,
> You're Mussolini,
> You're Mrs Sweeny,
> You're Camembert . . .

As debutantes, the Mitfords were less enthusiastic. Nancy remembers being presented and the only sanitary arrangement was a chamber-pot behind the screen. After her season she announced she was going to London to live in a bed-sitting room and study at the Slade. She cut off her hair, used lipstick, played the ukulele and invited her aesthetic friends from Oxford to stay. 'What a set!' Lady Redesdale exclaimed; sewers was what Lord Redesdale called them.

Her third sister Diana also brought a storm of rage upon her head by getting engaged to Bryan Guinness. The principal objection was that he was too rich. In the end her marriage was the most spectacular of the year and Lady Redesdale (who had once been called the penny-pinching peeress because she stopped using napkins, having calculated the cost of washing and ironing an average of nine, three meals a day, for 365 days a year) took no account of the expense.

Unity Mitford was a huge rather alarming debutante. She bought fake jewels at theatrical costumiers and wore them on immense brocade evening dresses. To her mother's dismay she crowned herself with a mock tiara, flashing with glass rubies, emeralds and pearls, stole writing paper from Buckingham Palace and took her rat with her to dances. Jessica was presented on the same day as Nancy, the latter on her marriage. She recalls the hairdresser coming to arrange their hair with feathers, the setting off in a hired Daimler, arriving, to inch through miles of slightly overfed human flesh, one girl thinking she was going to faint, another with her knickers falling down. Finally 'the Lady Redesdale, the Honourable Mrs Peter Rodd, the Honourable Jessica Mitford', and they were in the presence of what appeared to be two stuffed figures nodding and smiling down from their thrones like wound-up toys.

It seemed to Jessica that there was no time for anything except travelling from one function to another. The Bright Young People had faded away and there remained only a succession of lunches, teas, cocktail parties, dinners

Unity, Diana and Nancy Mitford.

and dances, with too little time to sleep in between. Dances were the main thing, taking place nightly, five times a week, with sometimes as many as three on one night. Endless successions of flower-banked ballrooms, filled with very young men and women resembling uniformly processed market produce at its peak with here and there an overripe or an underripe exception. Smooth fair guileless faces radiating the health bestowed by innumerable fresh air-filled upbringings in innumerable country houses.

For years at Swinbrook, Unity, Jessica and Debo had talked about what they would do when they were grown up. Unity said she was going to Germany to meet Hitler, Jessica said she was going to be a Communist and Debo said she was going to marry a Duke and be a Duchess—all three did exactly what they said they would do.

Communism was as great a threat to older members of the aristocracy as taxation. They disliked also what they called the Americanisation of the Prince of Wales—he had even picked up an American accent. His constant companion was Lady Furness, who had been presented by the American Ambassadress on the same evening as Margaret Whigham. She went down to Fort Belvedere most weekends and she and the Prince went for long walks dived into the swimming pool and worked at their sewing—for her birthday Queen Mary received a paperweight embroidered by her son's hand under the guidance of Lady Furness. It was in Lady Furness's house that the Prince first met Wallis Simpson, whose food was unrivalled in London. Lady Furness went off to California in 1934, and by the time she had returned six weeks later Wallis Simpson had taken over.

In January 1936 the King died at Sandringham. Mrs Simpson's name appeared in the court circular, dining at York House; she went aboard the S.S. *Nahlin* with the Mountbattens, the Duff Coopers and Lady Cunard as guest of the King; in August she went to Balmoral; in October she was divorced from Ernest Simpson—who had once tried to kiss Barbara Cartland in the back of a taxi. Lady Cunard was delighted, she saw Wallis Simpson as Queen of England and herself as Mistress of the Robes. The Archbishop of Canterbury was not. There would be no coronation if the King persisted in associating himself with a woman who had divorced two husbands. Families were split down the middle into those that believed that a modern king should please himself and those that saw the court in danger of being tarnished and Buckingham Palace becoming a sort of American nightclub. If the monarchy failed then the function of the aristocracy would wither and die. Lord and Lady Redesdale, who had by this time enjoyed a holiday in

Wallis Simpson in her presentation dress.

Germany being shown round by Unity and Hitler, were horrified by Wallis Simpson: 'Children!' Lady Redesdale exclaimed, 'you are not to mention that dreadful woman in front of the servants.' It was rumoured, furthermore, that the 'dreadful woman' was in league with the German ambassador, von Ribbentrop. Then suddenly the crisis was over. In December the King abdicated in favour of his brother.

George VI's coronation was a red letter day for the aristocracy. It was not Americans who were the new King's henchmen but the peers and peeresses of the realm. Queen Charlotte's Ball, the Courts, Ascot and Lords all came round again. At the Eton and Harrow match the crowd roared as an Eton wicket fell: *'Alors!'* enquired a bewildered Frenchman, *'c'est Harrods qui gagne?'* Lady Cunard's luncheons carried on—with von Ribbentrop among the favourite guests. But the tide of destruction had started. Twenty famous houses on the east side of Berkeley Square alone were demolished in 1937. In 1939, war was again declared. Now it was every man's duty to fight, on the beaches, in the streets, on and under the seas and in the air. And this time the destruction was appalling.

Chapter 11

PEACE came in 1945 and the following years were spent clearing up and struggling with clothes coupons and ration books. Girls came out all right, but they made their dresses out of bedcovers and drank cider cup. The coronation in 1953 was to be the beginning of the new glittering Elizabethan Era.

The Season was once more in full swing and this time I was one of the debutantes. We were not a vintage year. The structure remained unchanged from the thirties. First we went to tea parties to identify the other debutantes and towards the end of March the cocktail parties started so that we could examine our partners. We stood round in awful little cocktail veils and cocktail dresses, juggling with a cigarette in one hand and one's bag and drink in the other. After the party we all hoped to be asked out to dinner and be taken somewhere to dance—the Green Room perhaps, the Carousel, the Café de Paris or the 400. No one ever talked about money, the men paid, there was no question of going Dutch. People used to keep bottles of gin and whisky at the 400 so that the evening would only cost about ten shillings and one could get dinner and dancing at the Berkeley for £1.

The dances started on May 1 and went on every night until the end of July—London mostly during the week and the country at the weekends. Now the young men could live more or less free for the next three months, the only outlay being the laundry bill, which with six boiled shirts a week was substantial. One impecunious gallant compromised by covering his front with Blanco, which later in the evening transferred itself to his partner's bosom. One girl infuriated everyone by sending out invitations for a party at the end of the Season and a week before cancelling it—it was a well-known trick, everyone said, she never meant to give the ball in the first place. First you went to a dinner party and then on to the dance; the hostess was supposed to see that you got home all right and the men at the dinner party were meant to dance with you, but they could easily vanish. There was a special way of dancing, you leant slightly backwards, shoulders not moving, the right arm stretched down towards the floor, and if one was in love—or fast—the fingers were linked together. As the night wore on the men moved closer. There were no dance programmes. Music was continuous and the only way of changing partners was to go to the bar. There were stories of girls spending all night crying in the lavatory. Dances were held at places like the Ritz, the Savoy, the Dorchester, the Hyde Park, Hurlingham and Londonderry House which had a long narrow ballroom, and was not popular; dances there were too hot and crowded and one did not look forward to them. Lady St John of Bletso could also be hired, for presenting and chaperoning young ladies—she was to be seen in her tiara perching in an old-fashioned way on gilt chairs at the edge of dance floors.

My mother never chaperoned me. On the whole she was more interested in my clothes than my morals. 'I am determined you shall have a pink dress,' she said, so I did, pink chiffon with rose-petals, which soon got dirty. I was a disappointment to my mother, who would have liked to dress me up like a doll. For one thing she was cross with my hair—she had a fetish about hair. 'Now if you had hair like Caroline,' she would say—Caroline was a friend of mine with whom I came out, and who had curly hair. Mine was straight and I was forever curling and fiddling with it. One could never go out in the wind or rain in case the curls came out. Another bore was the foundation garments we wore, which we called stays. One was forever zipping oneself in and out of them. In the evening we wore sexy-looking things which nipped one in at the waist called Merry Widows. Girls who wore nothing under their evening dresses were considered very fast. Girls who slept with men were very fast indeed. Caroline and I used to discuss which debs went to bed with people. Some did and some did not—we did not. The most we did was to let them kiss us—in the backs of taxis, in their cars and in the bushes in the country. There was a code: N.S.I.T.—not safe in taxis. Some years later I fancied a handsome young meat millionaire. He took me out to dinner and back to my flat—a basement in Lennox Gardens—and the next thing I knew was that he had gone off with the girl I shared the flat with, literally into bed in the sitting room. I was furious, but there it was. She did. I did not—although it was more the fear of getting pregnant than any higher ethic.

I have a vision of myself at that time: silly certainly, noisy, rather shy, wild if given the occasion, pretty, I suppose—men working in bomb craters would whistle as I went by—but not, however, fast. I was surprised then

Curtseying to the cake at Queen Charlotte's Ball, 1952.

to discover letters from Caroline's brother (who was wonderfully good-looking, largely on account of his broken nose) written from Germany where he was doing his National Service. 'I can safely tell you that I shall miss you very much,' he wrote, 'as I think you were one if not the fastest deb I met this year . . .' A few weeks later he followed this up: 'I hear that your dance [at the Hyde Park] was a tremendous success and you looked absolute blissikins. I was misikins because I couldn't come . . .'

A few other relics remain from that Season. A list of 'Maids of Honour' for Queen Charlotte's Ball. The programme from the Caledonian Ball held, like Queen Charlotte's, at Grosvenor House, where my partners sound like a lot of hairdressers—my mother would have liked them. 'Strip the Willow' with Raymond, a *'valse'*, 'The Loveliest Night of the Year' with David; Paul and Clive figure a lot and 'Don't let the stars get in your eyes' was with John, one of the fastest delights of the year, decidedly N.S.I.T., having the reputation of deflowering several young ladies, including the friend with whom I was to share the flat in Lennox Gardens. Two days later there was the Herbert Sidon Debutante Collection. A lady called Mrs Ernest Simpson seems to have been on the committee, together with one called Madame Wabbla, and Hermione Gingold gave a talk on make-up. Goodness knows of what it was a collection—I can remember nothing about it at all, although apparently I was a model along with Fiona Campbell Walter. Maybe I missed it altogether, as I missed the coronation and Ascot, by being in bed with measles.

The summer passed in a daze of white ties, striped marquees and Tommy Kinsman's music. A few things stand out: a bathful of caviar at a party given at Albany by two disreputable delights, one of whom ended up in *prison*, and another delight who was in the Coldstream fainted from his hangover when he was supposed to be lining some route—he was in the newspapers photographed flat on his face and there was a terrible to-do. I can just remember being presented in pink—my mother again. Now, there were no evening courts and no ostrich feathers, no chamber-pots either, or knickers falling down. But Madame Vacani had taught me to curtsey at one of my schools: 'now, darlings,' she would say, 'throw out your little chests and *burst* your little dresses.'

Two years later I did the Season all over again in a much wilder way. I was living in Ovington Square with two friends and a couple of cats called Frankie and Johnny (our rent was £5 a week). An Italian starlet lived upstairs—or that is what the landlady called her. Her friends were certainly N.S.I.T. They had the noisiest orgasms I have ever heard. The landlady was always boasting about the starlet's exploits. We gathered that Tyrone Power was a frequent visitor and once had been so passionate he had broken the front door. This seemed very unfair, since the landlady made a frightful row if we so much as knocked down a light-switch. Down the road lived a wild and impoverished young man, with whom I was in love. Every morning we would look down the columns of *The Times* and see where the dance, and our dinner, was going to be. This time we really appreciated it—all that delicious food and drink and Tommy Kinsman still playing away. The larger and more lavish the affair, the more we liked it. And that year the dances were lavish. The more the hostesses spun elaborate webs to catch eligible suitors for their daughters, the more they caught us in their glittering threads. We became expert gate crashers. We sipped champagne in Hawaiian glades, underwater caves and woodland bowers fluttering with butterflies, we ate gulls' eggs on the shores of blue lagoons and tasted strawberries under ceilings of gathered tussore. Once an entire theatre was converted, stalls and all, into a gigantic dance floor for a thousand people, the boxes were crammed with flowers and

Tommy Kinsman.

the ceilings covered in black tulle. Sometimes we took parties. One girl (who, like the Mitfords, knew exactly what she was going to do, which in her case was to marry a peer and be the fashion writer of a well-known newspaper) made her entrance to a ball in Belgrave Square by sliding down the banisters. Next day there she was photographed in the *Evening Standard*, the hostess and legitimate guests hardly mentioned at all—there was a nasty scene after that. Later in the autumn we would dance at a club called the Condor. Georgie Brown would sing 'Sweet, sweet, the memories you gave to me,' everyone would get up to dance and we would go round drinking their drinks.

The whole thing came to an end when we moved. My wild friend made a bonfire in the garden of all our stays and then ran off down the road with our bras and pants. The starlet, who had been preparing herself against the night, appeared at the window. 'Darlings,' she shrieked, 'there are ten fire brigades in my bedroom!' She and a shadowy male figure were distanced by

Madame Vacani, the ultimate authority in the court curtsey.

Madame Vacani again: 'throw out your little chests
and *burst* your little dresses!'

several firemen who emerged with hatchets and hoses and sprayed our smouldering stays.

Individual presentations stopped in 1958 but the Season continued unchanged into the mid-sixties. Ballrooms were converted by bird-song and box-hedges into gardens at Versailles. Waitresses were dressed as witches and waiters as skeletons. One girl passed out at her dance and another had her name repeated at intervals up the drive in neon lights. Paul Getty had a dance with a funfair and one friend told me that at his sister's party the guests ate all the moss decorations surrounding the gulls' eggs. Another time they were sitting round the breakfast table, which was laid in the conservatory, after a dance in the country and a loaded chamber-pot crashed through the roof and landed in the grapefruit juice. Papers reported that 'the bright young things' were standing on the balconies of Londonderry House, pelting the passers-by with champagne, cushions, plates of kidney and cigarettes. One girl who came out in 1963 says that by then the Season had hardly any point, it was merely the herding of cattle into a marriage market and it had a nasty snobby side to it too—everyone was busy calculating the father's income from the clothes his daughter wore and the party that was given for her.

By the second half of the sixties it was in decline. People blamed the Socialist government, changing tastes or merely shortage of money. Barbara Cartland's son, Ian McCorquodale, thinks the rot set in when people stopped wearing white ties and stumped round in dinner jackets. But by 1967 Nigel Dempster says people were not even wearing black ties, they just arrived in whatever they were wearing. Hardly anyone was drinking either, except for himself. It was all sex and drugs. People smoked joints at Queen Charlotte's and there is a story of a survey conducted in the mid-sixties revealing that sixty percent of the debs had lost their virginity by Goodwood. It was the pop revolution. There was a new class image and pop stars were the new élite, the whole of society was mostly made up of restless rootless people with no connection to the soil, spending most of their time in cities.

Harold Nicolson saw in his lifetime the removal of eight emperors, twelve kings and fifteen minor dynasties. Our monarchy has survived two world wars and a social revolution and still stands as a symbol of unity, security and continuity—even if the mystique is somewhat diluted by television and Willie Hamilton. The Silver Jubilee Year was a mixture of patriotism and debunking; 'Land of Hope and Glory' was played at village fêtes and dances all over the country; fireworks, bonfires and royal processions filled the skies and the streets; there were Jubilee mugs and matchboxes, ties saying 'Stuff the Jubilee' and songs—one of which was called 'Fuck the Jubilee'. At one party, given to see the royal progress down the river, a wax dummy of

The last deb ever to be presented.

Her Majesty gazed out of the window and waved as the Queen floated by.

William Hamilton admits that under Elizabeth I he would have been in the Tower. The monarchy, he says, is the human equivalent of the London zoo, running at a greater cost and giving less pleasure than the chimpanzees' tea party; the House of Lords is a political geriatric unit and as for the Honours List it is a gargantuan trough into which everyone tries to get his snout. The Queen holds fourteen investitures a year and presents some 2,000 orders, decorations and medals. According to Hamilton, the O.B.E. is as common as sliced bread and there is a rumour that medals for the Victorian Order are made on a production line in Neasden out of obsolete railway lines. 'Today it is footballers, cricketers and brain-damaged boxers,' he says, 'we will not have long to wait for decorated bingo players.'

Our difficulty according to Peter Laslett, in *The World We Have Lost*, is that we want contradictory things: a system both of status and of universal social equality. 'Our Society is marked by a search after status and symbols to express it. Most important is a personal title.' A peerage, according to William Hamilton, is a convenient way of emasculating those whose presence in the government has become an embarrassment and for rewarding those whose political careers are finished; 226 life peers were created between 1958 and 1973. A knighthood is coveted by Tory M.P.'s, especially by their wives—Lady sounds so much nicer than Mrs. Behave yourself or say goodbye to that knighthood is the theory. Harold Macmillan, says Hamilton, was like a political Casanova. Knighthoods or peerages were given to any Tory M.P. who showed signs of life, averaging one a month between January 1957 and October 1963.

The British rejoice in snobbery, a trait illustrated by the following story. 'His wife,' a county lady announced to a friend of Lord Kinross's, 'is a Wallop [the family name of the Portsmouths]'. 'Dear me,' the friend replied vaguely. Afterwards he said: 'What is a Wallop? I ought to know. Is it some kind of albino or hermaphrodite or what?' Certainly our modern press loves a title as much as it loves money. The recent news that the Duke and Duchess of Windsor would hire themselves out to Palm Beach hostesses to lend a touch of class to their parties was a nice coup. The contents of only two of William Hickey's columns reflect the modern brand of snobbery. On 13 October 1977, he visited *Le Privé*, the newest nightclub, designed to become the capital's most exclusive joint—the social committee included one of Princess Margaret's ladies-in-waiting, a property developer's wife and the tycoon behind Carmen Rollers, and aimed to recruit exclusively rich people who are beautiful. Meanwhile in the same paper Jean Rook, after a Gala Gucci fashion show, had attended the party 'where everyone was on the guess list'. 'Romantic

By the second half of the sixties the Season was in decline.

Roddy Llewellyn', 'loosely linked with Princess Margaret', 'blood-heating Bianca Jagger', 'recently very loosely linked to her husband Mick', and 'at the table's lovely head' Margaret, Duchess of Argyll. The main topic appeared to be the press—and what a nuisance it was. 'I've stopped worrying about gossip,' the Duchess of Argyll told Jean Rook. 'You should try having the Press staked round your house for two days peeping through your kitchen windows.' Cameras flashed all through dinner. 'Is it like this always?' Jean Rook wanted to know. 'It happens everywhere you go except the bathroom,' Bianca Jagger told her.

Next day William Hickey was outside the Berkeley Hotel and a white Rolls Royce glided up and out stepped Barbara Cartland (seventy-five), a 'vision of loveliness in pink' and her son on their way to celebrate his fortieth birthday—all paid for by Barbara Cartland's former publisher, Victor Temlin (U.S. lawyer). First they shared a bottle of champagne, then adjourned for lunch where William Hickey noticed they had another bottle of champagne and two helpings each of caviar, then the men had roast beef and Barbara Cartland nibbled at noisettes of lamb. The bill, said William Hickey, was

£103. Afterwards they repaired to the Mayfair salon of 'royal couturier' Sir Norman Hartnell where she was fitted for a new dress in 'Barbara Cartland' pink. Cost £400.

Although the subject of spending money is dear to the gossip columns there is now a puritanical stigma attached to spending it irresponsibly. Modern debs are schooled to play down the money factor. What with the swivel eyes of the Inland Revenue and the risk of bombs being thrown into the soufflé, coming out, according to a recent article in the *Sunday Telegraph*, is now conducted with the undercover strategy of an atomic submarine slinking out of a Scottish loch. However, after four cups of Lapsang Souchong tea at an Eaton Mews party, one girl revealed to the *Sunday Telegraph* plans of a dance for 400 in Berkshire with Juliana's discothèque, champagne and breakfast—the marquee alone costing £1,000. But the star ball of the Season was the one at Blenheim, estimated by the *Sunday Telegraph* to cost £10,000. Taxation has for the most part put an end to such lavish parties. To keep their places these days people are turning them into opera houses, safari parks and motor car museums. Betty Kenward (who has now stopped publishing her debutante list) noted in 1974 twenty-four dances and seventeen cocktail parties—a far cry from those years when there was one a night and sometimes more from April to July. In 1977, even Queen Charlotte's was abolished, and the only dance Lady Diana Cooper had been to lately was given for her god-daughter to entertain Andy Warhol and was full of freaks. Deb's delights are mourning the delicious dinners and drinks. The last straw, one told the *Sunday Telegraph*, was when he went to a party at Hurlingham and was offered wine or beer.

So what is happening to the Season? Has it any point nowadays? Plenty of ex-debs think not. As recently as the fifties it was the only way to meet people. A girl at school still led a cloistered life, preparing herself for the whirl through society which should land her at the altar. But marriage is no longer the only career open to young ladies and divorce is increasingly popular. Who needs chaperones now we have the pill? The Season as a marriage *bourse* has become obsolete. According to Nigel Dempster, Fulham is populated by girls in their early thirties, with two children, whose marriages have petered out.

Peter Townend, the modern entrepreneur, is less sceptical and claims optimistically that the Season is alive and well. Indeed people are always asking him if *anyone* can do it. He looks through Debrett and sends memos to families with nubile daughters suggesting that they might be thinking of coming out. He can make or break a modern deb: he decides whether she is to be featured in the *Tatler* with the most eligible escort of the Season, circulates a list of marriageable young men, and superintends the mothers' lunches.

It would seem that snobbery is as intrinsic to the British as it ever was when Elizabeth I was rampant, or James sold titles in return for gold, but that it has become functionless, islanded, its meaning uprooted and divorced by an egalitarian society. What has happened is best reflected by the revived *Tatler*; the cover is unchanged but the glossy pages are no longer filled with the *haut-monde*. 'Hooray Henries' and 'Henriettas' are squeezed in between interviews with rock stars: 'Now when Torquil Trumpington and Lady Jane Jelloid share a giggle on the stairs they have a sneaking suspicion that the joke may be on them.' It all depends on your sense of humour.

Afterword

A friend sent me these notes on the contemporary New York Season, which seems a whirl of activity. Before Thanksgiving there is the Junior League Ball where green feather fans are distributed to all debs; at Christmas there is the International Debutante Ball with the girls prostrating themselves in the famous Texas curtsey—taught by a doyenne in Texas—a 'flamboyant-to-the-floor-dip' that leaves the crowd breathless; around the same time is the Infirmary Ball. Last year the debs' escorts complained that the fathers were pinching their behinds—in the old days (c.1950) they would have pinched the debs; it is now apparently *à la mode* to do it to the escorts. Besides evening balls there are *thé dansants*. Last year the President and Members of the Governing Board of the International Garden Club held their nineteenth presentation reception on the 26th November at half after four o'clock 'to honor the Debutante Daughters and Granddaughters of the Members and to benefit the Partow-Bell Landmark Fund, Pelham Bay Park, New York'. Music by Dutch Wolff. The house, my correspondent writes, was nineteenth-century, cold and draughty. Pink Carnations and roses garlanded the fireplaces and the 'mums' had done the flower arrangements. 'Mums', says my correspondent, should not do flower arrangements. The guests were W.A.S.P. (White Anglo-Saxon Protestant), and most had made their dresses with appropriate results. The mothers wore white gloves which they put on as a sign of respect when the girls, each carrying pink carnations in a spill, came into the room. Although it was billed as a tea dance, there was no tea: bourbon, which ran out, was served and 'uggy champagne'. To eat: watercress sandwiches, pizzas, balls of steak tartare and pigs in blankets. Dutch Wolff played undistinguished fanfares for each deb as her own and her parents' names were announced. Each deb curtseyed to the audience who were seated throughout the house on folding chairs. Most, it seems, had not taken advantage of the Texas doyenne; they were very wobbly and had to be supported by their fathers who tried to look as if they were on a golf course. My correspondent had further details supplied by her neighbour's commentary such as:

'They lost all their money in the Depression.'

'That one was caught in the pro shop of the club with a joint.'

'Her grandmother married the contractor on her house but he isn't so bad and she's darling.'

'That one just got in last year and we don't know about her.'

and so on and so on.